FP

FREE PRESS
PAPERBACKS

FREE PRESS PAPERBACKS
Published by Simon & Schuster
New York   London   Toronto   Sydney   Singapore

Founding Father

REDISCOVERING GEORGE WASHINGTON

by

RICHARD BROOKHISER

FREE PRESS PAPERBACKS
A Division of Simon & Schuster Inc.
1230 Avenue of the Americas
New York, NY 10020

First Free Press Paperbacks Edition 1997

FREE PRESS PAPERBACKS and colophon are trademarks
of Simon & Schuster Inc.

Designed by Carla Bolte

Manufactured in the United States of America

10   9   8   7   6   5   4   3   2   1

Library of Congress Cataloging-in-Publication Data

Brookhiser, Richard.
    Founding father : rediscovering George Washington / by Richard
Brookhiser.
      p. cm.
    Includes index.
    ISBN 0-684-82291-1
        0-684-83142-2 (Pbk.)
    1. Washington. George, 1732–1799.   2. Presidents—United States—
Biography.   3. Generals—United States—Biography.   4. United
States.   Continental Army—Biography.   I. Title.
E312.B85   1996
973.4′1′092—dc20
[B]   95-50650
                                             CIP

FOR ROBERT BROOKHISER, JR.

Contents

Acknowledgments

Twenty years ago I took a course from Garry Wills on Jefferson, which first interested me in Washington. Ronald Paulson and Richard Duncan let me write the essays that eventually became the Introduction.

William B. Allen gave me early encouragement. I also wish to thank my agent, Michael Carlisle, and my editors, the late Erwin Glikes, and Adam Bellow.

INTRODUCTION

Four of John Trumbull's paintings of the American Revolution hang, vast and remote, over the heads of tourists in the rotunda of the Capitol in Washington, but to see the complete series, in its original small scale and up close, you must visit the Yale University Art Gallery in New Haven, Connecticut. The depictions of George Washington that are included in the series are not the only good portraits of him, but they are the best historical portraits: images that put him in context. What they say about him, and (by implication) ourselves, is still worth pondering.

Yale's Trumbulls hang on a red wall in front of a green plush banquette meant to suggest an overripe art gallery of the past century. It is best to study the paintings in the order of the events they depict. The first two are pictures of battles: the failed American defense of Bunker Hill (actually Breed's Hill) in June 1775, and a failed American attack on Quebec six months later. As a young staff officer, Trumbull had been on

1

the margins of both conflicts: he had watched the battle of Bunker Hill through field glasses, from Roxbury to the south, and he had reported on the condition of American survivors of the Quebec campaign when they fell back to upstate New York the following summer: "I did not look into tent or hut in which I did not find a dead or dying man," he wrote in his memoirs.[1] The central event in each of Trumbull's re-creations is a military pieta, the death on the field of an American general, though both deaths are obscured in swirls of confusion and activity. Swords and rifles scatter like the spokes of broken wheels. Hands wave, lifeless limbs sprawl, flags stream or tangle crazily against smoky, lowering skies.

The third picture in historical order, *The Declaration of Independence,* is probably the most familiar (it is reproduced on the reverse of the two-dollar bill). But it is not a very good painting. Trumbull shows the drafting committee presenting its handiwork to John Hancock, but he was also obliged to include forty-odd additional Founding Fathers. There may be some interesting way to depict what is essentially a large committee meeting, but Trumbull has not found it. The heads of the seated and standing politicians are lined up like sardines in cans, and the unguided eye roams from John Adams's stockings to Thomas Jefferson's red waistcoat to the drum hanging oddly on the room's rear wall.

With *The Capture of the Hessians at Trenton,* the series suddenly changes, in two ways. For the first time, Trumbull gets to paint an American victory: the battle of Trenton, fought the morning after Christmas, 1776, was the first break in a long string of demoralizing defeats. He has also made a very different kind of painting. Once again we see a dying officer, for the Hessian colonel surrendering at center stage is mortally wounded. But this painting has a center of attention, and it is not the stricken but the mounted American general who extends a magnanimous hand—George Washington. The elements of the picture converge on Washington like the pieces of a kaleidoscope falling into a pattern. The cloud behind his head, lest we miss the fact of his preeminence, is white. Washington dominates all but one of the remaining scenes in the set, which concludes with his resignation as Commander in Chief. He wins the battles, the war, the peace, and the paintings.

The gallery has grouped the pictures around another, larger canvas, not strictly in the series but proclaiming the same message: a standing portrait of Washington after the Battle of Trenton, in a golden uniform and navy blue frock coat. Trumbull wanted to show Washington's generalship "in the most sublime moment of its exertion," and the moment he picked was a week after the Hessian surrender. The British had regrouped and retaken Trenton, and they believed, with good reason, that they had got Washington in a trap. Fifteen years later, Trumbull got Washington, now President, to pose for him, and to relive the moment. "I told the President my object; he entered into it warmly, and, as the work advanced, we talked of the scene, its dangers, its almost desperation. He *looked* the scene again, and I happily transferred to the canvass . . . the high resolve to conquer or to perish."[2] Washington escaped from the trap; if he had not, the new country might well have perished. Behind him, on the canvas, a horse rears and a cannon lies shattered; enemy campfires twinkle in the distance. But he radiates a majestic calm. An empire, one feels, might well break on that forehead or a republic arise.

Trumbull had personal reasons for his interest in the founding of the United States and for making his account of it spin, like a solar system, around the figure of George Washington, for he was politically engaged to a degree unthinkable in a modern American artist. After he left the army, he performed assorted diplomatic services for the United States in Europe, while his father and one of his brothers both served as Governor of Connecticut and both were close political allies of Washington. But Trumbull was also a professional painter. He wanted to make money from prints and copies of his works and from commissions. His clients included individual subscribers, patriotic societies, and Congress (whence the oversized copies in the Capitol Rotunda). His view of George Washington was more than a private vision. It was meant to sell, and it sold as well as it did because it was widely shared. For Trumbull and his contemporaries, Washington was the founder and the father of his country.

The first town to take Washington's name was Stoughtonham Township in western Massachusetts, in the spring of 1776. Americans had begun christening their sons after him the summer before. One of the multitude of courtesies that Washington had to perform in his correspondence was to thank parents who had given his name to yet another newborn. (Letter to Joseph Reed, July 4, 1780: "In offering my respects to Mrs. Reed, I must be permitted to accompany them with a tender of my very warm acknowledgments to her and you . . . for the honor you have done me in calling the young Christian by my name.")[3] The honors continued after his death. Capital, monument, and state appeared during the nineteenth century. Even now, he decorates the dollar bill and the quarter and helps Abraham Lincoln hawk cars during Presidents' Day sales (in democracies, vulgarity is a form of honor). A 1981 poll of American historians gave Washington third place among the presidents, after Lincoln and Franklin D. Roosevelt—down from second place in a 1948 historians' poll, but still high after almost two hundred years.

Yet there has been, if not a diminishing, a distancing. It is as if in moving from the gallery wall to the Capitol Rotunda, Washington has moved away from us. He is in our textbooks and our wallets, but not our hearts. We have discarded the cherry tree and the other tales of Parson Weems, but we have replaced them with little that moves or even informs us. Looking at the lips clamped firmly over the false teeth (we *do* know he had false teeth) we impute coldness to him, and we respond to him coldly. The Washington Monument anticipated the abstractness of the honor he is now paid. Here is no larger-than-life image, teetering on the edge of kitsch, as in the Lincoln or Jefferson Memorials. Inside the monument, the stairwell is particular and detailed, lined with inscribed blocks that the mid-nineteenth-century subscribers thought would be displayed in a temple-like structure. But these stone tributes have been hidden in a marlinspike, or a stylized spine, modernism ahead of its time, lean, clean, and impervious.

Washington's remoteness is partly his doing, partly ours. He wanted to put a gap between himself and his contemporaries. At the end of his second term as president, Mrs. Henrietta Liston, the wife of the British ambassador, told him that she could read the pleasure he expected from retirement in his face. "You are wrong," Washington insisted, "my countenance never yet betrayed my feelings."[4] Mrs. Liston scoffed at this (though not to him), for she had several times seen his countenance betray his feelings about public affairs. And there had been occasions, on battlefields or in caucus rooms, when Washington had let his feelings show, to inspire or persuade. But it was also true—and it became more and more true, as his reputation and his responsibilities increased—that he followed a policy of concealing his hand. He did this for reasons of prudence—so as not to commit himself prematurely, when his commitments carried more clout than anyone else's on the continent. He also kept his mouth closed lest he say something angry. Controlling his anger was a lifelong, and never wholly successful, struggle. He lost his temper in Cabinet meetings, once in Congress, once—spectacularly—in battle. Still he kept reining it in.

His contemporaries knew what his silences meant. "Thousands have learned to restrain their passions, though few among them had to contend with passions so violent," said Gouverneur Morris, a young colleague. They honored Washington's self-control; the knowledge that they were dealing with powerful latent forces added to their awe. The first serious biography of Washington, John Marshall's, treated him formally even in his cradle, describing "The Birth of Mr. Washington."[5] But with time, we have forgotten the effort his self-control required. We treat what was a result as a natural condition, as if Washington had been carved from the same stone as his monument.

Washington's reserve frustrates our cravings for emotional intimacy and personal detail—cravings that generate their own misconceptions of him. The appetite for closeness has become insatiable in the age of *People* and Oprah, of kinder, gentler presidents who feel our pain. But the impulse is much older. The first unserious biography of Washington, by Mason Weems, assumed that the personal preceded the political. "It *is* not, then, in the glare of *public,* but in the shade of *private life,* that we are to look for the man. Private life is always *real* life. Behind the curtain, where the eyes of the million are not upon him, and where a man can have no motive but *inclination,* no incitement but *honest nature,* there he will always be sure to act *himself:* consequently, if he act greatly, he must be great indeed."[6] Hence Weems's collection of intimate vignettes, especially those concerning Washington's childhood: his father's joy when he confessed that he had accidentally chopped the cherry tree; his father planting seeds which grew up to spell "GEORGE WASHINGTON" in the family garden, so as to demonstrate by analogy God's design in the universe. The only problem with these stories is that, in order to tell them, Parson Weems had to first make them up, since we know very little about Washington's education or his father.

Modern humanizers of Washington have taken a different tack. If private virtues cannot flesh him out, then perhaps private temptations will. In 1877 a handful of letters between a young George Washington and Sally Fairfax, a neighbor, came to light. Washington met her in his late teens, a decade before he married Martha Custis. But Sally Fairfax was already married, to one of Washington's in-laws (her husband was the brother-in-law of George's half-brother). The youthful letters are coyly romantic, and in his old age Washington wrote Sally that "the happiest" moments of his life had been spent in her company. Modern historians have spent many happy moments of their own on the correspondence, seeing the truncated relationship it suggests as a pattern for later political rectitude. "What anguish he must have suffered, any young man can imagine," wrote Samuel Eliot Morison in 1932. "It was a situation that schooled the young soldier-lover in manners, moderation, and restraint." When later calls to duty came, Washington's nature had been "disciplined . . . by philosophy and a noble woman."[7] This is not made up out of whole cloth like the cherry tree story, but it is still a stretch. The surviving letters are ambiguous: they could be passionate or flirtatious. Mrs. Fairfax burned most of the letters in her possession. Was that because they contained embarrassing revelations? Or revelations that would have been embarrassing only to people who had already come to think of their sender as a man who had been "Mr. Washington" in his cradle? Since Mrs. Fairfax was two years older than Washington and from a more sophisticated family, it is possible that she meant the friendship in a lighter vein than he took it. But that, like Morison's docudrama, is only speculation.

For two hundred years debunkers have looked for details that were purely embarrassing. The most considerable attack came during Washington's lifetime, from the transplanted

English radical Thomas Paine. Paine's earliest American journalism had expressed his admiration for his new country and for its Commander in Chief. At the start of the French Revolution Paine moved on to France. When he ended up in jail, narrowly escaping the guillotine, he felt the American government had not exerted itself to release him, and in 1796, he wrote a bitter open letter to Washington. The attack destroyed Paine's reputation in the United States, but it set one theme for later debunkers: that Washington was a bad general, whose strategy consisted of "doing nothing."[8] It is true that General Washington seemed to do nothing for long periods, and that he lost more battles than he won. But as any student of military history knows, that begs the question of whether he was a successful general. The fact that Washington had critics during his lifetime is now presented as something scandalous, a gee-whiz item for Sunday supplements. Washington was the only man to win a unanimous vote for president in the Electoral College, not once, but twice. Yet he had enemies in the press besides Paine, and given the journalistic standards of the day—far shoddier than our own—they wrote lively copy.

Another favorite revelation of debunkers has been that Washington was a rich man, who keenly sought to make himself richer. He was born to prosperous gentry, he worked for rich neighbors who introduced him to the land business, and he married the richest widow in the colony. No log cabins in this life story. Washington's drive for wealth knew some bounds: for the last twenty years of his life, he refused to sell a slave. Sex with the slaves he kept has been a more meager theme, since there is so little for even the malicious to go on. Sir Arnold Toynbee once told a journalist that everyone knew Washington died from a cold caught while sneaking to his slave quarters. But no one knew this except Sir Arnold. The national libido has had to divert itself with Thomas Jefferson and Sally

Hemings. If the debunkers have done no lasting damage, they have kept up an annoying buzz.

We are especially susceptible to trivializing arguments today, whether well or ill intentioned. If Washington's contemporaries were too willing to be awed, we are not willing enough. We are simultaneously too ethereal and too down-to-earth. As idealists, we believe that ideas are self-enacting. We think them, therefore they are. Thus the American Revolution was a triumph of democracy or the enlightenment (or American imperialism or patriarchy). As reductionists, we believe that the historical figures, who floated like chips in the intellectual backwash, attached themselves to the cause for trivial motives, often sordid. We have lost the conviction that ideas require men to bring them to earth, and that great statesmen must be great men. Great statesmen are rare enough in this world. We believe they are mythical, like unicorns.

The humanizers have done even more damage to Washington than the debunkers, because they distract from the most important issues in his life. They assume that the career is not interesting enough. It is as if we thought that founding a nation was a routine task, an easy call. "Washington didn't do something big, it's just he was first," said a ninth-grader on Long Island, interviewed after Richard Nixon's funeral. (Nixon was "memorable," the student added, because "many American jobs depend on Chinese relations.")[9] It is hard to imagine how even a ninth-grader could believe such a thing these days. In the two hundred years since the American Revolution, many countries have transformed themselves, many more have been founded, and most of these efforts—from the French Revolution to the last offensive in Bosnia—have been disappointing, when they have not been disastrous. It would be wrong to jeer at the failures of other peoples, many of whom have labored under burdens of history, oppression, or ignorance, which made success a faint prospect. Though crimes are never excusable, failure may be inevitable. Still, the record of so many dashed hopes should give us pause.

Nor should we be too smug about ourselves. Of course Washington succeeded, we tend to think, look who he had to work with. Jefferson, who wasn't there, called the Constitutional Convention an "assembly of demigods," an attitude that has been enshrined in words like "framers" and "founders," used with implicit reverential capital *f*'s. Certainly the talent level in America at the end of the eighteenth century was high. When one reflects that Washington, as President, in preparing his third annual message to Congress, took suggestions from Jefferson and James Madison, sent them to Alexander Hamilton to be worked up, and finally gave the draft to Madison for a rewrite, one then turns to any presidential speech-writing team of the last sixty years (including Nixon's) and weeps. But talent isn't everything. Even the best can fail, because the best are men. If men were angels there would be no need for government, wrote Madison, and he had reason to know, since at many moments in his long political career, he showed himself to be rigid, arrogant, or ineffectual. The same could be said of most of his brilliant peers. And their bad moments were far from the worst that the leadership class of the young country supplied. Benedict Arnold and Aaron Burr (both survivors of the battle of Quebec) were also patriots. This makes Washington's achievements all the more remarkable. If he had been taken by smallpox or dropped by an Indian bullet as a young man, the future United States might well have come into being in some form or other. But it would have been harder, and it might have been a lot harder.

Parson Weems was wrong: we must look for the man in the glare of public life. His deeds are enough to do him honor. Any one of them would have guaranteed him fame; the series, the variety of the series—military, constitutional, political—and the span of time it covered—twenty-four years, from taking command of the army until his death—make a unique record. As with the blessings shown to Israel during the Exodus, the service rendered at each step of his career, from the age of forty-three on, would have been enough, but there was always another step and another service, as long as he lived.

What follows is not a life history of George Washington, but a moral biography, in the tradition of Plutarch, of Washington as a founder and father of his country. It is organized in three sections. The first surveys what he did during the Revolutionary War, the debate over the Constitution, and his presidency. The first chapter in the section examines the military turning point of the war and the ways Washington kept the American military obedient to him and to Congress. The second chapter shows how he helped bring about a transformation of the American government, from the Articles of Confederation to the Constitution, without a second revolution and in a way that made it acceptable to opponents of the change. The third chapter focuses on two crises of his second term, one domestic and one foreign, which tested the United States' commitment to self-government (the country passed the tests, largely because of Washington's commitment). The chapter and the section end with his final service, which was to retire. Unlike Julius Caesar or Augustus—whose careers the American revolutionaries knew well—or Napoleon—whose career was soon to come—Washington neither assumed a crown nor became a leader-for-life.

The second section seeks to explain why Washington was able to do what he did by looking at his nature, his morals, and his ideas. It covers many details of his private life, but only if they relate to his public career. It is not important to Washington's public career who his siblings were (with one exception) or what his stepchildren were like. It is important that he was over six feet tall, that he liked the theater, and that he subscribed to ten newspapers. Nature made Washington physically imposing and hot-tempered. His manners and his morals kept his temperament under control. His commitment to ideas gave him guidance. Washington's relation to ideas has been underestimated by almost everyone who wrote of him or knew him, and modern higher education has encouraged this neglect. It is the intellectuals around him—Jefferson, Madison, Hamilton, Benjamin Franklin, even John Adams—who make the curriculums and the reading lists. But Washington followed what they wrote with care; several of them wrote at his behest. His attention to courtesy and correct behavior anticipated his political philosophy. He was influenced by Roman notions of nobility, but he was even more deeply influenced by a list of table manners and rules for conversation compiled by Jesuits.

The third section explores the implications of political "fatherhood." Americans started thinking of Washington as the father of their country even before there was a country: a correspondent called him a "political father" in January 1776.[10] The title involved ironies and questions: ironies, because the nation's father had no children; questions, because the title did not of itself settle what kind of a political father he would be. (George III was also the father of his country; so, in our day, was Papa Doc Duvalier.) The title has become ever more problematic, as we have come to doubt what fathers are and what they do. The contemporary failure of fatherhood is perhaps the subtlest barrier to our understanding of Washington, the greatest source of the distance between us and him.

Closing the gap is not an academic exercise. Moral biography has two purposes: to explain its subject, and to shape the minds and hearts of those who read it—not by offering a list of two-hundred-year-old policy prescriptions, but by showing how a great man navigated politics and a life as a public figure. Plutarch's *Lives of the Noble Grecians and Romans* was very popular with eighteenth-century Americans; they knew something about the power of example that we have forgotten. When he lived, Washington had the ability to give strength to debaters and to dying men. His life still has the power to inspire anyone who studies it.

Career

WAR

The state begins in violence. However lofty the ideals of a new country or a new regime, if it encounters opposition, as most new regimes and countries do, it must fight. If it loses, its ideals join the long catalogue of unfulfilled aspirations.

At six o'clock on the evening of July 9, 1776, the soldiers of the main American army, stationed in New York, were paraded and read the Declaration of Independence. General George Washington, Commander in Chief, hoped this "important event" would inspire them, though when some soldiers joined a mob in pulling down a statue of George III, he deplored their "want of order."[1] Over the next two months, the American army and its commander, orderly or not, were unable to offer much in defense of the Declaration's sentiments.

Washington had done well in his first posting. The previous summer, he had taken command of the New England militias encamped around Boston, which was occupied by a British army. The American position was strong. The battles of Lexington, Concord, and Bunker Hill, all fought before Washington arrived, had established that the British were unable to break out of Boston, then a tadpole-shaped peninsula projecting into Boston harbor. Once he placed captured British cannon on the Dorchester Heights overlooking the town, the enemy evacuated. Now the geographical situation was reversed. New York then occupied the tip of Manhattan Island, surrounded by an undefendable harbor, and flanked by Staten and Long Islands. The Americans had no navy to prevent the enemy from landing wherever they chose.

During the summer, the British assembled, on Staten Island and in the harbor, the largest expeditionary force of the eighteenth century: ten ships of the line, twenty frigates, and 32,000 regular troops. On August 22, most of these troops began moving to Gravesend Bay on Long Island, in what is now southwest Brooklyn. Anticipating a possible landing there, Washington had posted more than a third of his own force of 19,000 men on Brooklyn Heights, and on a line of hills to the south. But he expected the British to attack him on the harbor side of his position, where they could bring the guns of their ships into play. On the morning of the 27th, the British slipped a force through the hills five miles away in the opposite direction and hit the American front line from before and behind. "It is impossible for me to describe the confusion and horror of the scene that ensued," an American veteran wrote years later: "the artillery flying with the chains over the horses' backs, our men running in almost every direction, and run which way they would, they were almost sure to meet the British or Hessians." Many of the retreating Americans had to cross a swamp at Gowanus Creek, now the Gowanus Canal. "Some of them were mired and crying to their fellows for God's sake to help them out; but every man was intent on his own safety and no assistance was rendered." Washington rallied the survivors on

Brooklyn Heights and managed to convey them to Manhattan on the foggy night of the 29th: a skillful retreat, but retreats do not win battles or boost morale. The Americans had lost five hundred killed, and a thousand captured. "I fear Gen. Washington has too heavy a task,"[2] wrote one American officer.

For two weeks, the British did nothing. Some of Washington's officers wanted him to abandon New York, and Nathanael Greene, one of the youngest and the best of them, suggested he burn it. But he held on to Manhattan even as he made preparations to leave it, stationing divisions at opposite ends of the island and a string of troops in "lines" along the East River—though, as one militiaman who was posted at Kip's Bay (now the east 30s) remembered, the lines "were nothing more than a ditch dug along on the bank . . . with the dirt thrown out towards the water." Looking out at the river at dawn on September 15, this soldier saw five enemy warships and many transport boats, whose number increased until the red-coated soldiers on board "appeared like a large clover field in bloom." An hour before noon, the warships opened up a broadside: "I made a frog's leap for the ditch," wrote the American, "and began to consider which part of my carcass was to go first."[3]

The bombardment continued for two hours, then the British brought the troops ashore. This time, there was no slaughter, for the Americans ran, without firing more than token shots. "The ground was literally covered with arms, knapsacks, staves, coats, hats" abandoned by retreating soldiers, the militiaman wrote (he had been retreating himself). When Washington heard the cannonading at his headquarters in Harlem, five miles away, he rode toward the point of the landing and tried to get some units to defend a wall, a cornfield, any part of rural mid-Manhattan, but soldiers and even officers would run pell-mell or stand briefly, then run at the sight of fresh enemies. There are several accounts of what he cried out in his chagrin: "Good God, have I got such troops as those?" runs one version; "Are these the men with which I am to defend America?" runs another. Certainly the letter he wrote Congress the next day glows with the embers of shame and anger. ". . . to my great surprize and mortification I found the troops that had been posted in the lines retreating with the utmost precipitation and those ordered to support them . . . flying in every direction, and in the greatest confusion, notwithstanding the exertions of their generals to form them. I used every means in my power to rally and to get them into some order; but my attempts were fruitless and ineffectual; and on the appearance of a small party of the enemy, not more than sixty or seventy in number, their disorder increased, and they ran away in the greatest confusion, without firing a single shot." He was not just losing, he was losing ignobly. There were other low points for George Washington in the war, but this was low enough. After the last Americans had fled, a listless Washington had to be led away from the approaching redcoats by an aide; so "vexed" was he, wrote Greene, that "he sought death rather than life."

The British agreed with his judgment of the situation. "The dastardly behavior of the rebels," the admiral's secretary wrote in his journal, "sinks below remark."[4]

Washington had been named Commander in Chief by the Second Continental Congress, meeting in Philadelphia in June 1775. He was forty-three years old. There was not yet any American army for him to command, only the militias ringing Boston, but the delegates of the increasingly rebellious colonies were seized by a fury for action and for war. "Oh that I was a soldier," wrote John Adams, a radical lawyer from Massachusetts. "I will be. I am reading military books. Everybody must and will, and shall be a soldier."[5] Adams never became a soldier, but Washington had already been one. He had served in the Virginia militia during the French and Indian War twenty years earlier, rising to the rank of colonel. In his old age, Adams would describe Washington's selection as a political compromise—a southern commander, to lead what would at first be a mostly New England force—engineered by congressional wisemen, including Adams. But Congress did not have many other officers to choose from. Israel Putnam, of the the Connecticut militia, was, at 57, too old. Artemas Ward, the commander of the Massachusetts militia, was incompetent and suffering from the stone. Charles Lee, an Englishman-turned-rebel, had been a major in the regular British Army and a major general in the service of the King of Poland. Intelligent, opinionated, and odd—his closest companions were a pack of dogs, particularly a Pomeranian named Mr. Spada—Lee was one of those eccentrics who can cause reasonable people to think that their very waywardness is proof of their gifts. But he was handicapped not only by his foreign birth but by his demand that Congress compensate him for the English property he expected to lose by joining the American side.

Washington was not just chosen by process of elimination. First among his positive qualifications for the job was his political commitment to the cause. Not an obvious radical—he was a rich planter—he resented the newfangled controls Britain was fastening on its American colonies, as did many of his peers. Virginia was one of the most radical of the colonies— Massachusetts opposed British policies because a British army had been occupying Boston since 1768; Virginia felt anger even at a distance—and Fairfax County, where Washington lived, was among the most radical counties in Virginia. The local ideologist, George Mason, was another wealthy planter, and a neighbor of Washington's. Thomas Jefferson (who was then less famous than Mason) remembered him as "a host" in debate, "strengthened by a dash of biting cynicism." But Mason had one drawback as a political leader—a reluctance to hold office. So Washington presented resolutions written by Mason to the Virginia legislature, which called for support of Massachusetts and for a continental congress. While Washington was attending the first Congress in the fall of 1774, Fairfax County organized a militia of its own, "hoping to excite others by our Example." Washington was elected commander. At the Second Continental Congress in 1775, Washington headed four committees on military matters and supplies. "Coll. Washington," wrote Adams, ". . . is of much service to Us."[6]

He cut an impressive figure, a combination of noblesse oblige and modesty. Charles Lee might worry about compensation. But Washington would offer to serve without pay, asking only that Congress cover his expenses. Rumor magnified his magnanimity: the Virginian, it was said, had proposed to outfit one thousand men at his own expense. Washington had outfitted one man, himself: he attended Congress wearing the uniform he had worn in the French and Indian War, which he had designed. Yet he managed to wear it without a trace of braggart's swagger. "He seems discreet and virtuous," wrote one delegate, "no harum-scarum, ranting, swearing fellow, but sober, steady, and calm."[7]

But the main qualification for his new appointment was his reputation from the French and Indian War. The old war, as it came to be called, had been the final struggle between Britain and France for control of the Continent, and Washington took part in some of its most dramatic moments; indeed, he had fired the first shots in it. In 1753, before the war began, Washington, a major in the militia with training as a surveyor, made a three-hundred-mile trip into the Pennsylvania wilderness to scout out French intentions, keeping a journal which was published in Virginia and London. He was only twenty-one years old. In 1754, he went back into the woods at the head of a small force, where he attacked a party of French. "I heard the bullet's whistle," he wrote a younger brother, "and, believe me, there is something charming in the sound." When this was printed in a London magazine, King George II remarked that "he would not think so if he had been used to hear many." In another letter, Washington wrote that he expected to drive the French to Montreal; instead, they surrounded him and forced him to surrender. Britain's agent for Indian affairs felt the young officer had been "too ambitious of acquiring all the honour," and hence overly impetuous.[8] But the colonial consensus was that Washington had been outnumbered by enemies who had been up to no good.

In 1755, Washington witnessed a far greater defeat, when an army led by British General Edward Braddock was cut to pieces outside Fort Duquesne, now Pittsburgh. Washington, who was serving as Braddock's aide, had two horses shot out from under him, led a remnant of men to safety, and buried his slain commander. Americans shocked by the debacle fastened on Washington's survival. The Reverend Samuel Davies, a Presbyterian minister, speculated that Providence had preserved him "in so signal a manner for some important service to his country."[9] Washington spent three more years commanding the Virginia militia on the frontier, angling (in vain) for a better assignment and seeking (successfully) to maintain the discipline of his troops.

Washington's fame twenty years later was based on the Braddock campaign; Davies's sermon was reprinted in a Philadelphia newspaper in 1775. But his record was more complex than his reputation. Washington was unquestionably brave. His conduct during Braddock's defeat was not the only instance; on one night march, when his soldiers accidentally fired on each other, he stepped between their blazing muskets and struck them up with his sword. He was also tough. Throughout Braddock's last battle, he was sweating with a fever. Though he came to resent the privileges enjoyed by officers in the regular British army, who outranked militia officers of the same grade, he valued regular discipline and had the faculty of instilling it in his men. "You took us under your tuition," his officers wrote him when he resigned his commission, and "trained us up in the practice of that discipline which alone can constitute good troops. . . ."[10] His desire for honor was a mixed quality. It could make him wayward, but it was also the engine of his efforts.

Washington's greatest weakness in the old war was his lack of a strategic sense. His first battle was a collision of scouting parties, and his other assignments, including his stint with Braddock, consisted of aide's work or service in sideshows. Like many a soldier before and after him, he thought his front was the whole conflict. But the war was won elsewhere and by other means, by battles hundreds of miles away, and by Indian diplomacy. There was no reason why a militia officer in his twenties should have understood the big picture. But the leader of a continental rebellion would have to acquire the skill.

When Washington accepted his commission as Commander in Chief, he told Congress, with a sincerity that was partly justified, that if "some unlucky event should happen unfavorable to my reputation, I beg it may be remembered by every gentleman in the room, that I this day declare . . . that I do not think myself equal to the command I am honored with."[11]

Several elements of the picture that faced the new commander in 1775 favored the enemy. Britain had the strongest credit of any nation in the world. The British Army, though corrupt and brutal, was a professional force. The mother country had many sympathizers in the colonies and many more potential sympathizers, who might become active if it looked like winning. Most important, for three years, the British would have complete command of the seas—and America was well suited to naval invasions. Every state except Pennsylvania had an Atlantic seacoast, and Philadelphia could be reached by oceangoing vessels coming up the Delaware River. The greatest potential enemy of the British was distance—the distance across the Atlantic, which made reinforcement slow and costly, and the distances of America itself. But some way had to be found to make these count against them.

The war played itself out in four theaters. It began in New England and ended in the South, and upstate New York saw several important campaigns. Washington commanded briefly in the first two theaters and observed northern New York from afar. But he spent most of the war in the fourth, the central theater, a hundred-mile stretch between New York and Philadelphia. The shuttle flies over it in twenty minutes. There, from the summer of 1776 to the summer of 1778, he fought seven battles and won only two of them. But during that time, he managed to solve the strategic problem. Though by the end of 1778 he had not won the war, he had made it unwinnable for the enemy.

He had notions of what it would take to accomplish this, even as the British were squeezing him out of New York. The first requirement was regular soldiers and officers, trained and disciplined so that they would not follow a defeat like Long Island with a rout like Kip's Bay. This meant long enlistments and a Congress willing to shoulder the expense. State militiamen, who signed up for short terms during the excitement of 1775, were not enough. "When men are irritated and the Passions inflamed," he wrote the President of Congress from Harlem, "they fly hastily and cheerfully to Arms; but, after the first emotions are over, to expect, among such People, as compose the bulk of an Army, that they are influenced by any other principles than those of Interest, is to look for what never did, and I fear never will happen."[12]

Since he did not have such troops at hand—much of his time and energy over the course of the war would be spent cajoling Congress to supply them—the strategy he adopted was defensive. "We should on all occasions avoid a general action, and never [be] drawn into a necessity to put anything to the risque . . . I am sensible a retreating army is incircled with difficulties; that declining an engagement subjects a general to reproach . . . but when the fate of America may be at stake on the issue . . . we should protract the war, if possible." This was true enough. If Washington's army were destroyed, the cause would not recover, and delay, and the increased expense arising from it, told more heavily against the British. But Washington at this point thought an effective defensive strategy could be fought defensively, by maintaining a series of fortifications or "posts": "I have never spared the Spade and Pick Ax."[13] He did not yet see that troops in posts could not hit the enemy or understand how hard the enemy could hit them; his education in the weakness of posts had only begun.

Meanwhile, the events of the summer weighed upon him. "[I]f I were to wish the bitterest curse to an enemy on this side of the grave, I should put him in my situation," he wrote a cousin. "I see the impossibility of serving with reputation. . . . In confidence I tell you that I never was in such an unhappy, divided state since I was born."[14]

The day after the landing at Kip's Bay, a British force, approaching Washington's headquarters on Harlem Heights, caused a small party of Americans who were observing them to retreat, whereupon a British bugler derisively played a fox-hunting call. "I never felt such a sensation before," wrote one of Washington's aides, "it seemed to crown our disgrace."[15] What Washington, a passionate fox hunter, thought of it is not recorded. What he did was to throw the British back with losses, in the "battle" of Harlem Heights, actually a skirmish. But early in October, the British outflanked him by sailing up the East River and landing in his rear on the mainland, forcing him to leave Manhattan. At the end of the month, the two armies came to battle in White Plains, where the Americans had fortified the high ground, but the British captured ground that was higher, and Washington retreated again.

He crossed the Hudson and turned south down its western shore to a second post, Fort Lee. As the weather turned colder—there had been snow on the eve of the battle of White Plains—troubles cascaded on him. He had left fifteen hundred men in a third post in northern Manhattan, named Fort Washington, and Nathanael Greene advised him that they could hold out. Washington agreed. But the British captured the fort named after him on November 20. Four days later they crossed the Hudson, hoping to trap the Fort Lee garrison between the Hudson and the Hackensack, a stream to the west. The only escape route was one narrow bridge, and the Americans fled over it.

Charles Lee, for whom the abandoned fort had been named, had stayed with half the army north of White Plains. Lee was coming to have a low opinion of the abilities of the sometime militia colonel. So were others. "Oh! General," one of Washington's own aides now wrote Lee, "an indecisive mind is one of the greatest misfortunes that can befall an army; how often I have lamented it in this campaign!" "Indecision . . . in war," Lee agreed, "is a much greater disqualification than stupidity, or even want of personal courage." Lee did not say whether indecision was worse than insubordination. He had been urging that Massachusetts militia units earmarked for the main army be sent to him, instead of the Commander in Chief. "There are times when we must commit treason against the laws of the state for the salvation of the state," he had written in explaining himself. "The present crisis demands this brave, virtuous kind of treason."[16]

The New Jersey countryside through which the subject of this correspondence was retreating was the least suited to a war of "posts": flat farmland, no hills to dig in on, no stone fences for bulwarks. It was also populated by Quakers, who were unwilling to help the army out of pacifist principle, and Tories, who wanted the other army to win. Washington fell back and back. On December 12 came more bad news: Lee, moving south from White Plains through New Jersey at a leisurely pace, had been spotted by the British at an inn where he was sleeping and captured by a party of dragoons. Washington had already left the state, crossing the Delaware River into Pennsylvania. This crossing was fully as grim as the famous one. The painter Charles Willson Peale met one soldier "in an old, dirty blanket jacket, his beard long, and his face so full of sores he could not clean it." Not until the soldier spoke did Peale recognize him as his own brother.[17]

Thomas Paine, who had accompanied the army from Fort Lee, scribbling notes by campfire-light, using drumheads as desks, hurried to Philadelphia to print a pamphlet, called *The American Crisis*. "There is a natural firmness in some minds which cannot be unlocked by triffles, but which, when unlocked, discovers a cabinet of fortitude; and I reckon it among those kind of public blessings, which we do not immediately see, that GOD hath . . . given [General Washington] a mind that can even flourish upon care."[18] There were cares enough. The enlistments of Washington's militia would run out on January 1st; the British were offering pardons to all in New Jersey who would rally to the crown and finding many takers. Now was the time for Washington's genius to flourish, if he could summon it.

Trenton, on the Jersey side of the Delaware, only thirty miles from Philadelphia, was the foremost British post, held by Hessians. The Hessians celebrated Christmas vigorously and were sluggish the next morning. They had also been deceived as to American intentions by the testimony of a supposed Tory spy, actually an American agent (Washington was a great believer in spies and disinformation). Washington planned to ferry his army across the Delaware on Christmas night in three divisions. Because of snow and ice, two turned back. One was enough. After the brief clash, an American soldier remembered, the two dozen dead Hessians looked like "sheaves of wheat lying in a field over which the reapers had just passed."[19] Nine hundred of their comrades were taken prisoner. Only two Americans had been wounded; one of them was Lieutenant James Monroe.

The Americans went back over the Delaware, justly pleased with themselves. "This is a glorious day for our country,"[20] Washington told an officer. Yet if he had gone into winter quarters at that point, it would have been a day of glory and no more. The British would have retaken the town the Hessians had lost, the campaign would have ended with all of New Jersey in enemy hands and Philadelphia threatened, and the Battle of Trenton would merely have been a raid. Washington needed to strike a second time.

First, he needed to persuade his militiamen to extend their service. Half a century later, a former sergeant remembered Washington addressing his regiment thus: "My brave fellows, you have done all I asked you to do, and more than could be reasonably expected. . . . You have worn yourselves out with fatigue and hardships, but we know not how to spare you. If you will consent to stay only one month longer, you will render that service to the cause of liberty and to your country which you probably never can do under any other circumstances."[21]

Whatever Washington's exact words, the sergeant's reconstruction of them included no appeals to "interest." Yet interest was served: Robert Morris, a Philadelphia financier, rushed Washington fifty thousand paper dollars for soldiers' bonuses and a bag of hard currency for spies. When Washington had made sure of his army, he crossed the Delaware for the fourth time that month and took up a position just outside Trenton on a hill across a creek named the Assunpink. A small force of artillery and guards held the town.

Not for long. On the second day of the new year, a substantial British force moved down from Princeton, ten miles away, and entered Trenton at dusk. The Americans fell back over the Assunpink. "The bridge was narrow," one of them wrote later, "and our platoons were . . . crowded into a dense and solid mass, in the rear of which the enemy were making their best efforts." At the far end of the bridge, "the noble horse of General Washington stood with his breast pressed close against" the rail, "and the firm, composed, and majestic countenance of the General inspired confidence and assurance. . . . At the end of the bridge, I pressed against the shoulder of the General's horse and in contact with the boot of the General. The horse stood as firm as the rider, and seemed to understand that he was not to quit his post and station."[22] Encouraged by his commander, so did the soldier.

This was the situation John Trumbull tried to evoke nineteen years later. There was a British army at Washington's feet, besides a garrison in Princeton and other British forces scattered across the state. The war council Washington called decided not to try to defend themselves, as the Americans had done at Long Island, White Plains, and Fort Washington, but to forgo the war of posts and strike into enemy-controlled territory. Leaving their campfires burning, they made a night march along back roads that took them finally to Princeton.

"We moved slow on account of the artillery, frequently coming to a halt, or stand still, and when ordered forward again, one, two, or three men in each platoon would stand, with their arms supported, fast asleep; a platoon next in the rear advancing on them, they in walking, or attempting to move, would strike a [tree stump] and fall."[23] Because the route was indirect, the march covered twenty miles. By sunrise, the Americans were approaching Princeton; the fields shone with frost.

A British sergeant, later taken prisoner, said the men in Princeton "felt as safe as if we had been in the kingdom of heaven." So it was a surprise when several hundred British grenadiers, leaving town to join the main army in Trenton, encountered a smaller party of American riflemen coming toward them. The two units met in an orchard. "Dress [line up] before you made ready," an American officer shouted. "Damn you, we will dress you," the enemy answered.[24] British infantry tactics relied on bayonets rather than firepower, since a well-disciplined soldier could outrun the range of a musket in the time it took an enemy to reload. So it was now: after the first volleys, the British charged and came upon the Americans before they could get off a second shot. General Hugh Mercer, the American senior officer, was bayoneted seven times; Lieutenant Bartholomew Yeates of the 1st Virginia regiment was stabbed thirteen times. The surviving Americans fell back from the orchard to a second road, where they ran into the main body of their own army coming up. Fresh troops and bloodied troops milled in confusion.

Now the "noble horse" and its rider, so stolid the night before, were all motion. Washington put his troops in line, then led them toward the British. "Parade with me, my brave fellows," one remembered him calling. When they were thirty yards away, he gave the command to fire. Colonel John Fitzgerald, a staff officer, pulled his hat over his eyes, lest he see Washington fall. When he pulled it away, the British line had broken and Washington was unhurt. Fitzgerald wept with relief; Washington clasped his hand, then rode after the fleeing British, crying, "It is a fine fox chase, my boys."[25]

It was Washington's answer to the bugler on Harlem Heights. It was also the end of the beginning. Washington wintered in northern New Jersey, while the British withdrew toward the coast. The following summer, the British army put to sea, landed on the northern shore of Chesapeake Bay, and marched overland to Philadelphia, which they took after beating Washington at Brandywine Creek in September. Twenty-three days later, Washington attacked the suburb of Germantown in a dense fog. Though he lost again, the French foreign minister declared that "nothing struck him so much" as two battles waged so closely together, by a raw force. Since they were accomplishing nothing by holding Philadelphia, the British marched out in June 1778. Washington caught up with them at Monmouth Courthouse, New Jersey, on a day of hundred-degree heat. This battle ended the career of Charles Lee, who had been released in an exchange of prisoners. Lee was assigned to make the first assault but pulled back, believing himself to be outnumbered. One of his soldiers who kept a diary agreed: "thay being so much Superior to our Number we retreated . . . a Number of our men died with heat a retreating." Washington did not agree. Appearing on the field, he asked Lee the cause of "all this disorder and confusion." Lee stammered; then, according to one account, Washington swore "till the leaves shook on the trees. Charming! Delightful! Never have I enjoyed such swearing before or since. Sir, on that memorable day, he swore like an angel from heaven." The soldier who "remembered" this profanity had not actually been there, but certainly Washington, at long last, had had enough of Lee. (Lee described himself as "disconcerted, astonished, and confounded by the words and the manner in which His Excellency accosted me." Washington's manner, Lee added, was "much stronger and more severe" than his words.) After dealing with Lee, Washington took charge and fought the battle to a draw. He "seemed to arrest fortune with one glance," wrote the Marquis de Lafayette, a young French officer who had been on Washington's staff for a year. ". . . His presence stopped the retreat." ". . . by his own presence, he brought order out of confusion, animated his troops, and led them to success," agreed Alexander Hamilton, an immigrant from the Caribbean who was also on Washington's staff. "Other officers have great merit in performing their parts well, but he directed the whole with the skill of a master workman. . . . I never saw the General to so much advantage." The British retired to New York.[26]

Two years earlier, Washington had been planning to wage a war of "posts." Now the British were in a post, which they had first won in the fall of 1776. "It is not a little pleasing nor less wonderful to contemplate," wrote Washington, "that after two years maneuvering . . . both armies are brought back to the very point they set out from, and that that which was the offending party in the beginning is now reduced to the use of the spade and pickaxe for defense."[27]

In achieving this result, Washington had not just won, or drawn, a campaign. By confining the main British army to New York City, central New Jersey, and Philadelphia for two years, he had destroyed whatever strategy the British possessed. At the beginning of the war, London had counted on the rebels to fight like amateurs and on loyal Americans to rally in large numbers to the cause of the crown. If the first had happened, the second would certainly have occurred. In the best case, the British hoped to win a quick victory by annihilating resistance at a stroke. Failing that, they might have rolled up the important colonies piecemeal. Washington knew, from the very beginning, that he must keep his army from being destroyed and keep it in the field. What he learned in the crucial half year from Long Island to Princeton was that he had to keep it in the field, alternately hitting the British and retiring beyond their reach. In the nature of things, he had to fight a defensive war. But by fighting an aggressive defensive, which was also fluid, he raised the cost of victory for the British to an unacceptable level. With four thirty-thousand-man armies—one for each major theater—Britain could have won a war of strangulation. But Britain could not maintain four thirty-thousand-man armies three thousand miles from home.

The war lasted four years and four months after Monmouth Courthouse. France had come in on the American side in February 1778, offering troops, supplies, and above all seapower. From 1780 to 1781, Britain focused on the south, a campaign that Nathanael Greene won with Washingtonian tactics, fighting six battles and losing five, but ultimately driving the British to Yorktown, where Washington commanded the final victory. But Washington had first changed the strategic equation.

Military buffs have a weakness for classy losers—Rommel, Robert E. Lee, Napoleon. But the purpose of generalship is to win wars. If you are a prodigy or a genius, an Alexander or a Caesar, then you bring victory from whatever you touch. Washington was not in that class. But a successful general does not have to be the best general in the world. All he has to be—or if he is not so already, all he has to become—is better than the generals he faces.

The enemy is not the only threat a commander faces, if he fights on behalf of a nation of laws. The army may become a law unto itself, especially if the government is capricious or incompetent. When Washington wrote the President of Congress from Harlem in September 1776 to plead for a regular army, he added that "the Evils to be apprehended from one, are remote; and in my judgment, situated and circumstanced as we are, not at all to be dreaded. . . ."[28] Having offered this reassuring judgment, he was obliged to uphold it, on three separate occasions during the remainder of the war.

Soldiers can turn on their governments as individuals, for reasons of personal ambition or gain. During the flight across New Jersey in 1776, Charles Lee had speculated about "virtuous" treason—insubordination in the service of the cause. The great example of virtue-less treason occurred four years later; the soldier who supplied it was one of the best in the American army, Major General Benedict Arnold.

As a fighter and a leader, Arnold was a natural. In the fall of 1775, he took a thousand men overland from the Maine coast to Quebec City; the journey took twice as long as expected, and the Americans lived on dogs, soap, and boiled moccasins. They attacked the city in a snowstorm; Arnold was shot in the leg. The next summer, when the British sent an armada down Lake Champlain, Arnold built a fleet of ships of his own design and turned them back. In the summer of 1777, the British invaded northern New York again, and the Americans stopped them, not with worthy defeats like Brandywine or Germantown, but with two crushing victories near Saratoga. Arnold, the second in command, "seemed inspired with the fury of a demon . . . the very genius of war"[29] and was shot in the leg a second time.

A variety of motives drew Arnold to treason. He resented Congress's slowness in promoting him. Washington intervened on his behalf: "Surely a more active, a more spirited and sensible officer fills no department in your army," the Commander in Chief wrote a congressman. "It is not to be presumed . . . that he will continue in the service under such a slight."[30] Arnold needed money, both because he had laid out thousands of dollars of his own to pay for the Quebec expedition and be-cause he enjoyed high life. In 1778, when he was acting as mil-itary commandant of reconquered Philadelphia, he fell in love with a fetching young Tory.

But the proximate cause of his betrayal was a clash with the civil authorities. Arnold, who had been a merchant before the war, continued trying to make money on the side while he was posted in Philadelphia, and he used his position to speed his investments. These activities—which, if not illegal, were cer-tainly injudicious—came to the notice of enemies of Arnold in the Pennsylvania state legislature who drew up a list of eight charges, which eventually came before Congress, and a court-martial.

When the process got underway, Washington told Arnold that he would have to go along with the investigations. Wash-ington had been having bad experiences of his own with politi-cians. After the first flush of military enthusiasm, many in Congress had begun to begrudge the expense of war. John Adams, who had once wanted to be a soldier, wondered why Congress should maintain "vast armies in idleness. . . ." After the loss of Philadelphia, Washington's critics had added an in-dependent Inspector General to the command structure and filled the post with an Irish-born French officer, Thomas Con-way, who seemed to them "to possess [Charles] Lee's knowl-edge and experience without any of his oddities and vices." Conway had vices of his own, however, and lasted only four months. By 1778, Washington had come to feel that Congress was filling up with second-raters. Benjamin Franklin had gone to Paris as a diplomat, where Adams would soon follow. Jeffer-son had returned to state politics in Virginia. "Our political system may be compared to the mechanism of a Clock," Wash-ington wrote. ". . . it answers no good purpose to keep the smaller wheels in order if the greater one which is the support and prime mover of the whole is neglected." But he trusted that Arnold would be justly dealt with, and when the court-martial finally ratified only two of the original charges and sentenced him to nothing more than a reprimand, Washington, in May 1780, tempered it with praise: "The Commander in Chief would have been much happier in an occasion of bestowing commendations on an officer who has rendered such distinguished services to his country as Major General Arnold; but in the present case, a sense of duty and a regard to candor oblige him to declare . . ."[31] Arnold had already been in contact with the British for eleven months.

The plot he finally matured was to turn over West Point—a post worth holding, since it controlled the Hudson River. The plot collapsed when Arnold's British handler, riding alone through Westchester county at night, was captured by three men who may have intended to rob him, but who patriotically handed him over to the Americans instead. Arnold fled, leaving his Tory wife behind. Colonel Hamilton wrote a letter describing what happened next. "The General went up to see her, and she upbraided him with being in a plot to murder her child. One moment she raved, another she melted into tears. Sometimes she pressed her infant to her bosom . . . in a manner that would have pierced insensibility itself." It was an act, to divert suspicion from herself, which Washington did not penetrate. Washington was an acute judge of generalship and a severe critic of incompetence ("as to [General] Sevier," he would write of one officer years later, "the only exploit I ever heard of his performance, was the *murder* of Indians"). But characters as unprincipled as the Arnolds were opaque to him. Mrs. Arnold ultimately joined her husband in exile. Arnold spent the rest of the war raiding his country, wrangling with the British over his reward, and offering advice, some of it strategically astute, some of it morally appropriate to the giver. "A title offered to General Washington might not prove unacceptable."[32]

Arnold's actions will preserve his memory as long as America lasts. But the disaffection of groups of soldiers could have had more serious consequences. In January 1781, two mutinies of long-suffering American troops occurred in rapid succession. The mutineers had genuine grievances. Conditions in their camps were barely human, which was chronic; they had not been paid for twelve months, which was not unheard of; and while they had signed up for three years or the duration of the war, thinking that meant whichever came first, when their three years ran out, they found that the authorities planned to hold them until whichever came last. The Pennsylvania line marched out of its barracks on New Year's Day, killing an officer in the confusion. But they kept good order otherwise and arrested two British agents who tried to tempt them to "turn . . . *Arnolds*."[33] The mutiny ended when the government offered back pay and furloughs. When part of the New Jersey line rebelled later in the month, Washington ordered them surrounded by loyal troops; the ringleaders were tried on the spot, and two of them were shot by their own comrades.

Washington's general orders after the New Jersey mutiny praised the "patience" and "Fidelity" of the loyal troops and condemned the mutineers for a "daring and atrocious . . . departure from what they owed to their Country, to their Officers, to their Oaths and to themselves." He also employed a measure of shame: "History is full of Examples of armies suffering with patience extremities of distress which exceed those we have suffered, and this in the cause of ambition and conquest . . . shall We who call ourselves citizens discover less Constancy and Military virtue . . . ?" Shame was not reserved for the troops alone, however, for Washington used the occasion to try to prod the civil authority into redressing the men's grievances. Their "calamities and distresses . . . are beyond description," he wrote the governors of the New England states after the first mutiny. "The circumstances will now point out much more forcibly what ought to be done, than anything that can be said by me, on the subject." His fundamental consideration was what it had been at the onset of Arnold's legal troubles: legitimate authority must be obeyed. If soldiers could "dictate terms to their country . . . civil liberty" would perish.[34]

The worst disorder in an army occurs, not when the privates mutiny, but when the officers do. Officers, by definition, are used to wielding power. If they disobey, it is not to overturn authority, but to assume it. As the war wound down, the threat that the army, led by its officers, might challenge the power of Congress was very real—and so, in some minds, was the hope that Washington might direct the challenge.

Washington's attitude toward Congress had been developed and prepared over decades. When he served in the French and Indian War, he had quarreled and intrigued with colonial governors and legislators over promotions and assignments. Sixteen years in the House of Burgesses, the lower house of the Virginia legislature, plus his experience in the Continental Congress, had educated him in the political process. This is not to say that after he put on a uniform again in 1775, he awaited Congress's instructions passively. Washington was constantly requesting, cajoling, and complaining; his official correspondence was voluminous, urgent, and often desperate. Reading it for the first time, someone who did not know the outcome of the war would be assured of the army's continued existence only because new warnings of its impending dissolution kept being written.

Yet Washington never crossed the line that separates entreaty from compulsion, or even the threat of compulsion. His letter to the New England governors after the first mutiny is typical. After pointing to the "calamities and distresses" of his troops, he gets down to business. "It is not within the sphere of my duty to make requisitions, without the Authority of Congress, from individual States: but *[but what?]* at such a crisis, and circumstanced as we are, my own heart will aquit me; and Congress, and the States . . . I am persuaded will excuse me *[is he going to make a requisition anyway?]*, when once for all I give it decidedly as my opinion *[no, he is not]*, that it is in vain to think an Army can be kept together much longer . . . unless some immediate and spirited measures are adopted . . . *[He ticks them off—food, clothing, and three months' pay—then goes on in his scrupulous way.]* I have transmitted Congress a Copy of this Letter, and have in the most pressing manner requested them to adopt the measure which I have above recommended, or *[giving them even more leeway]* something similar to it, and as I will not doubt of their compliance, I have thought proper to give you this previous notice, that you may be prepared to answer the requisition." In 1782, the Chevalier de Chastellux, an author and *philosophe* who met Washington when he served with the French army in America, put Washington's relations with civil authority at the heart of his portrait of the man: "This is the seventh year that he has commanded the army and he has obeyed Congress: more need not be said."[35]

But from the beginning of his service, Washington was beset with people who wished to say more on his behalf. Popular adulation of the Commander in Chief was strongest during the revolutionary effervescence of 1775. Dr. Solomon Drowne, a congressman from Rhode Island, wrote home that he wished the contest could be settled in a single combat between Washington and George III. Phillis Wheatley, another Rhode Islander known as the "African poetess," wrote an ode ending, "A crown, a mansion, and a throne that shine/ With gold unfailing, Washington be thine!"[36] The long years of the struggle, while they gave rise to doubts and criticisms, transformed the infatuation into genuine admiration. And by war's end, some of the infatuation returned.

Lord Cornwallis surrendered at Yorktown, Virginia, on October 17, 1781, after a perfect conjunction of circumstances: a British army, hundreds of miles from any base, having been forced to cover long distances; a French naval blockade; a Franco-American siege. Peace negotiations began in March 1782. Soon thereafter, Washington received a curious letter from a Colonel Lewis Nicola, an Irish Huguenot. "Republican bigots will certainly consider my opinions as heterodox, and the maintainer thereof as meriting fire and fagots."[37] But "this war must have shown to all, but especially to military men in particular, the weakness of republicks." Shouldn't Washington become a king?

Such a bald suggestion could probably only have been made by a foreigner, and an ingenuous one at that. But the idea was not as peculiar as it now sounds, even for Americans. Shadowy approaches were made to various European royals during and after the war; John Trumbull, in his role as diplomat, may have been in touch with Charles Edward Stewart, the Jacobite pretender to the British throne. Nathaniel Gorham, who served as President of Congress in the mid-1780s, is thought to have asked Prince Henry of Prussia to become regent if the government collapsed. Five years after Colonel Nicola wrote, Hamilton—another immigrant colonel—would lecture the Constitutional Convention on the virtues of elective monarchies. Washington's answer to Nicola, though blunt as a bat, was directed not only at the colonel, but at whatever like-minded, less overt colleagues of his there might be. "Let me conjure you then," Washington concluded, "if you have any respect for your Country, concern for yourself or posterity, or respect for me, to banish these thoughts from your Mind, and never communicate, as from yourself, or anyone else, sentiments of a like nature."[38] Washington asked his aides for written confirmation that his reply had been mailed—the only time he did such a thing during the war. After he got this letter, the flustered Nicola wrote three apologies in as many days.

The threat to civil peace was not from amateur political scientists, but from disaffection among the officer corps as a whole. The cause, as for the mutinous soldiers, was money. The finances of the United States had been in chronic chaos since 1775. Congress had no power to levy taxes, only to make requisitions upon the states, to which they responded, as they could or would. Some states were still not entirely integrated into the cash economy; Virginia accepted tobacco in payment of taxes. There was no American hard currency; Americans used Spanish pieces of eight (whence the expression, two bits). Congress printed paper money, and kept printing it, which gave rise to another expression: "Not worth a continental." The states followed suit. American diplomats raised loans abroad, but as the country's finances deteriorated, this became more difficult. Congress tried to come up with some plan for paying the army what it was owed, but as the peace negotiations dragged on for months and into 1783, the army, quartered at Newburgh on the Hudson River, grew restive.

On March 10, an anonymous leaflet, from "a fellow soldier," circulated through camp, addressing their predicament. "If this, then, be your treatment while the swords you wear are necessary for the defense of America, what have you to expect from peace, when your voice shall sink and your strength dissipate by division?" The time for forbearance was past. If Congress offered any further indignities, "the army has its alternative": to "invit[e] the direction of your illustrious leader" and "retire to some unsettled country."[39] Another leaflet called for a meeting on the following day. Washington forbade the assembly, but scheduled an official one on the fifteenth.

Washington agreed with the substance of "a fellow soldier" 's complaint—soldiers should be paid—and with a part of his mind he believed that such considerations determined men's actions. "Men may speculate as they will; they may talk of patriotism; they may draw examples from ancient story, of great atchievements performed by its influence; but whoever builds upon it, as a sufficient Basis for conducting a long and bloody War, will find themselves deceived in the end. . . . For a time, it may, of itself, push Men to Action; to bear much, to encounter difficulties; but it will not endure unassisted by Interest."[40] But to answer the fellow soldier's argument now, Washington had to make an appeal beyond interest.

Washington's call for a meeting had implied that he would not attend, and when the officers gathered, he was not on the dais. But a side door opened, and he entered, as if on cue. (Washington had seen his first play when he was nineteen, and he remained a theatergoer all his life.) Washington began his remarks by accusing the fellow soldier of taking "advantage of the passions, while they were warmed by the recollection of past distresses, without giving time for cool, deliberative thinking. . . ." He then proceeded to summon the passions for his own ends.

He did it by establishing his common ground with his listeners, in a long series of parallel constructions, that are typical of his writing at its most engaged. "As I was among the first who embarked in the cause of our common Country." *[The first soldier commissioned by Congress had been the Commander in Chief.]* As I have never left your side one moment, but when called from you on public duty. *[In eight years, he had not furloughed himself.]* As I have been the constant companion and witness of your Distresses, and not among the last to feel, and acknowledge your Merits. *["This is a glorious day for our country," he had said after Trenton.]* As I have ever considered my own Military reputation as inseparably connected with that of the Army. *["I see the impossibility of serving with reputation," he had fretted in Harlem.]* As my Heart has ever expanded with joy, when I have heard its praises, and my indignation has arisen, when the mouth of detraction has been opened against it, it can *scarcely be supposed,* at this late stage of the War, that I am indifferent to its interests." Only after such a preamble did he arrive at "interests." Interests may be worthy things; they may be only another name for our desires, our needs, our rights. But they are not abstractions; to be real, they must be realized, fought for. Washington was reminding his listeners that he had fought with them and as hard as any of them.

His argument consisted of two points: the plan to retire to the wilderness was unrealistic, and Congress was not the enemy. The ex-Burgess explained how legislatures work. "Like all other large Bodies, where there is a variety of different interests to reconcile, their deliberations are slow. Why then should we distrust them?" He ended with the same word he had used in the conclusion of his letter to Colonel Nicola, "conjur[ing]" his listeners, as Americans, gentlemen, freemen, and soldiers. "In the name of our common Country, as you value your own sacred honor, as you respect the rights of humanity, and as you regard the Military and National character of America" do not "open the flood Gates of Civil discord, and deluge our rising Empire in Blood."

But there was one appeal he had made to Nicola which this catalogue had left out: "your respect for me." He drew on this, of course, in the famous gesture after he finished his speech. To demonstrate Congress's good intentions, he wished to read a letter. But he fussed with the paper and at last pulled on a pair of glasses. He had been forty-three when he became Commander in Chief; now he was fifty-one. "Gentlemen, you will permit me to put on my spectacles, for I have not only grown gray but almost blind in the service of my country."

But surely, the preparation for this appeal, and for the tears of the officers (rebels no more) that followed it, had come earlier in the speech. When had he last spoken of "service"? Twice: when he had referred, in his last paragraph, to their "faithful and meritorious Services," and in the paragraph before that, in a remarkable offer: "In the attainment of compleat justice for all your toils and dangers . . . you may freely command my Services to the utmost of my abilities." These three services were not just a verbal echo, but an emotional and a moral one as well. The Commander made them his commander; how could they then fail to do their duty?

After Washington left the hall, the meeting voted unanimously "that the officers reciprocated his affectionate expressions with the greatest sincerity of which the human heart is capable."[41]

Peace was finally concluded in September 1783, and Washington reentered New York, for the first time since he had been driven out of it seven years earlier. He went on to Annapolis, where Congress was sitting, and on December 23 resigned "with satisfaction the Appointment I accepted with diffidence. . . . Having now finished the work assigned me, I now retire from the great theater of Action."[42]

CONSTITUTION

Four years after Washington had left the theater of action, demonstrating his obedience to Congress, he reentered it, for the purpose of replacing Congress. In between, he enjoyed a brief interval of private life.

One of Washington's guests during this period, after admiring his champagne, his niece, and the grounds of Mount Vernon, visited his stables. "Among an amazing number of horses I saw old 'Nelson,' now twenty-two years of age, that carried the General almost always during the war. 'Blueskin,' another fine old horse next to him, now and then had that honor. . . . They have heard the roaring of many a cannon in their time. . . . The General makes no manner of use of them now; he keeps them in a nice stable, where they feed away at their ease for their past services."[1]

Washington felt himself at ease at Mount Vernon, though he was scarcely idle. Added to the chores of a planter were the burdens of fame. Artists wanted to take his likeness. "At first," he wrote, "I was as impatient of the request and as restive under the operation as a colt is of the saddle. The next time, I submitted very reluctantly, but with less flouncing. Now no dray moves more readily" to the shaft of his cart "than I do to the painter's chair." Visitors came from all over the country, from France the ally, and even from England the former enemy, occasionally more than ten at a time. Many of them bore letters of introduction, some dropped in unannounced: to reminisce, if they were veterans, or just to gawk. At least one arrived sick. His host "pressed me to use some remedies, but I declined doing so. As usual after retiring, my coughing increased. When some time had elapsed, the door of my room was gently opened, and on drawing my bed-curtains, to my utter astonishment, I beheld Washington himself, standing at my bedside, with a bowl of hot tea in his hand. I was mortified and distressed beyond expression." The state of Pennsylvania proposed that Congress make Washington an entertainment allowance, but he refused the offer. Those who could not come to Mount Vernon, wrote. When Washington complained of the volume of letters, his secretary observed that he chose to write back, whereupon Washington declared that his correspondents "must receive an answer of some kind."[2]

One project that engrossed him was the navigation of the Potomac. If a canal could be pushed over the mountains to link up with the Allegheny river system, then all the future produce of the Ohio Valley could flow through Virginia (and, not coincidentally, past Mount Vernon). A portage to Lake Erie would bring in the Detroit fur trade as well. Washington had helped push a Potomac canal bill through the House of Burgesses before the war; after the war, the Virginia legislature passed a second bill, chartering two new canal companies and presenting Washington with one hundred and fifty shares of stock in them, which he accepted only on the condition that any dividends would be given to charity. Hearing about the advantages and the prospects of the canal was a cost of staying at Mount Vernon. "The General sent the bottle about pretty freely after dinner," wrote one of his guests, "and gave success to the navigation of the Potomac for his toast. . . ." "To demonstrate the practicability" of the scheme, recalled another, "was his constant and favorite theme. . . . Hearing little else for two days from the persuasive tongue of this great man, I confess completely infected me with the canal mania." Washington's enthusiasm was stimulated when, on a visit to Warm Springs, the keeper of the boardinghouse where he stayed, one James Rumsey, drew him aside and showed him a model boat which seemed to be able to convert the force of the current into power to pole itself upstream. "The discovery is of vast importance," Washington wrote. Some of his acquaintances did not think it so vast. To James Madison, a young politician from western Virginia, Washington's absorption with the canal suggested a man whose wheels were spinning as idly as the poles of Rumsey's boat. ". . . a mind like his, capable of great views and which has long been occupied with them, cannot bear a vacancy."[3]

Rumsey's boat never worked, and the Potomac Company only paid one dividend, after Washington had died. But his embrace of the idea was neither eccentric nor fruitless. He was drawn to the plan by important private and public interests, and the political steps he took to fulfill it led directly to the Constitutional Convention, if not to a canal.

Washington was personally interested as a landowner. His family had first speculated in Ohio Valley land decades ago, and Washington owned nearly sixty thousand acres. In 1770, only a year after Daniel Boone first went to Kentucky, Washington had canoed down the Ohio River, hunting wild turkey and bison and surveying tracts to be awarded to French and Indian War veterans in what is now West Virginia. Washington assigned the best parcels to himself, an act he defended by arguing that he had done the work and borne the costs of the trip. In 1784, he revisited his property and tried, unsuccessfully, to rid it of squatters. A trans-Appalachian commercial artery would have been a windfall to him. More than a century later, his namesake, George Washington Plunkitt, a Tammany Hall functionary, hoped that his own epitaph would read, "He seen his opportunities, and he took 'em." Washington hoped to turn what he had taken into opportunities. Political scientist Glenn Phelps suggests that Washington made no mention of canals or the west in his valedictory messages as Commander in Chief precisely because he had such a large stake in them: "Washington wisely recognized that on matters related to the West he was rightly seen as self-interested. . . ."[4]

But Washington also believed that a canal would benefit other Americans besides himself, including people who were not yet Americans. His letters to friends on the potential of the Ohio Valley were written in that vein of boosterism that achieves its fervor only because it is sincere; in one epistle, to his protégé and fellow veteran the Marquis de Lafayette, he tapped St. Matthew, Moses, and Isaiah for promotional copy. "We have opened the fertile plains of the Ohio to the poor, the needy and the oppressed of the Earth; any one therefore who is heavy laden, or who wants land to cultivate, may repair thither and abound, as in the Land of promise, with milk and honey: the ways are preparing, and the roads will be made easy."[5]

Washington finally wanted a canal out of a concern for national unity. The idea, later christened "Manifest Destiny," that America would roll from the Atlantic to the Pacific like a carpet did not seem at all manifest in the 1780s. Quite apart from the British, the Spanish, the Indians, and other rival claimants to the continent, the extent of the country and the harshness of much of the landscape seemed to make it likely that America itself could split into at least two nations. Well into the nineteenth century, Americans assumed that the Great Plains, then known as the Great American Desert, would naturally divide the continent into two republics. For Washington, the potentially sundering barrier was the Appalachians. ". . . unless we can connect the new States which are rising to our view in those regions, with those on the Atlantic by *interest*, (the only binding cement . . .), they will be quite a distinct people." This could only be done by "mak[ing] it easier and cheaper for them to bring the product of their labour to our markets, instead of going to the Spaniards southerly"—via the Mississippi to Spanish New Orleans—"or the British northerly"—up the St. Lawrence, through Canada. If the states of the coast did not offer such an alternative, the western settlers could become "very troublesome neighbours. . . . In themselves considered merely as a hardy race, this *may* happen; how much more so, if linked with either [Spain or Britain] in politics and commerce."[6]

Before these political ends could be secured, practical political steps had to be taken—and these had far-reaching implications. Under the Articles of Confederation, the constitution that had been ratified during the war, each of the United States retained many semisovereign powers, including the power to charge for the use of its waterways. Even if it became possible to ship a load of pelts or a bargeful of wheat from the shores of the Great Lakes to the mouth of Chesapeake Bay, it might not be worthwhile if it were burdened with interstate taxes. In March 1785, Virginia and Maryland, the two states that border the Potomac, met to coordinate their common commercial interests. The meeting convened in Alexandria, Virginia, virtually on Washington's doorstep; midway through, the conference crossed the doorstep and concluded its business at Mount Vernon. The next year, Virginia invited all thirteen states to a convention to discuss commercial concerns. When the meeting was held in Annapolis in September 1786, though only five states showed up, they issued a call, written by Alexander Hamilton, now in civilian life, for another meeting in Philadelphia the following spring, to discuss not only commercial questions but "the situation of the United States."

The "situation of the United States" required attention for reasons other than transportation. Congress continued to labor under an unpayable load of debt. It still depended for revenue on requisitions from the states, which still mostly did not pay. Earlier in the decade, Congress had considered an amendment to the Articles of Confederation allowing the national government to charge a five percent tax on imports. Hamilton, a delegate from New York, and James Madison, who represented Virginia, had both supported the plan and become friends. But amendments required the consent of all the states, which Rhode Island would not give; while Rhode Island held out, Virginia withdrew its approval. "What, my dear Sir, could induce the State of Virginia to rescind its assent . . . ?" Washington wrote the governor testily. "How are the numerous Creditors . . . to be paid?" The two young congressmen quit in disgust. The creditors who suffered most from Congress's feebleness and poverty were veterans. At Newburgh, Washington had urged his officers not to distrust Congress, and in his final circular to the states, before resigning his commission, he reminded Congress of its obligations. Officers' pay "was the price of their blood and of your Independency, it is therefore more than a common debt, it is a debt of honor."[7] Yet the debt had not been honored, and many veterans had been forced to sell their back-pay certificates to speculators at a fraction of the nominal value.

Congress was not the only debtor. The states had run up debts of their own, which they tried to retire by issuing paper money and raising taxes. The taxes, especially land taxes, made debtors of their citizens, and in the summer of 1786, farmers in western Massachusetts led by Daniel Shays, a captain during the war, attacked courts to prevent foreclosures. Thomas Jefferson viewed the uprising with composure. ". . . what country can preserve its liberties, if its rulers are not warned from time to time, that [the] people preserve the spirit of resistance? . . . What signify a few lives lost in a century or two? The tree of liberty must be refreshed from time to time, with the blood of patriots and tyrants. It is its natural manure."[8] But Jefferson was viewing it from Paris, where he served as the American Minister to France. Closer to home, things looked significant indeed.

Washington got most of his information on Shays' rebellion from Henry Knox, the former commander of his artillery, who sent him alarming accounts of "twelve or fifteen thousand desperate and unprincipled men" scattered throughout New England, and "determined to annihilate all debts public and private." This was an exaggeration of the rebels' numbers and their intentions. But what most distressed Washington, as the stream of letters he wrote during the fall and winter of 1786 shows, was not the details of the upheaval, but the underlying political situation it revealed. The principle of self-government, which he had fought a war to secure, seemed to be threatened, for the rulers Shays and his followers were rebelling against were their own representatives. "It is but the other day that we were shedding our blood to obtain the Constitutions under which we now live; Constitutions of our own choice and making; and now we are unsheathing the sword to overturn them. The thing is so unaccountable, that I hardly know how to realize it. . . ." Washington felt he knew what the government should do. "Know precisely what the insurgents aim at. If they have *real* grievances, redress them if possible. . . . If they have not, employ the force of government against them at once." If the constituted authorities were unable to do either, then perhaps there was something amiss in the constitutions under which they operated. "That the Foederal government is nearly, if not quite at a stand, none will deny. The first question then is, shall it be annihilated or supported?"[9]

Washington did not propose to answer this question all by himself. In the run-up to the war, he had consulted closely with his neighbor George Mason, the sharp-spoken planter. Now, in addition to his fretful correspondence with Knox, Hamilton, Secretary for Foreign Affairs John Jay, and numerous others, Washington turned for analysis and advice to another Virginian, former congressman James Madison. Mason was eight years older than Washington; Madison was nineteen years younger, but he made up in brilliance what he lacked in experience. He had been educated at the College of New Jersey, later Princeton, a hotbed of prewar republican sentiment, and finished his degree in two years, after which he suffered a nervous collapse. When his health mended, he studied for another year and then went into politics. The experience of working with Hamilton to try to put Congressional finances on a firmer footing left him with a lively sense of Congress's impotence. During the winter of 1785–86, he attacked the problem in the manner most congenial to him, by immersing himself in a shipment of books he had asked Jefferson to send him from Paris. The price was $222, which in those days bought almost two hundred books.

The immediate result of Madison's labors was an analysis of the vices of the constitutions of ancient and modern confederacies. The examples were not encouraging. "The moment a cause of difference sprang up capable of trying [the] strength" of the Swiss confederacy, "it failed." The United Netherlands, which had given America financial help during the war, was marked by "imbecility in the government; discord among the provinces; foreign influence and indignities," and was in fact falling apart as Madison wrote.[10] He followed his history lesson with a detailed proposal to remedy the vices of the constitution of the United States, which he produced in March 1787 and shared with Washington and other like-minded Virginians.

Washington's preoccupation, during the winter of 1786–87, was to decide whether or not to attend the Philadelphia convention. When the Virginia legislature chose him to be one of the state's delegates in December, he wrote the governor that "circumstances" would all but surely prevent him from going. To Madison, he explained the circumstances. The Society of Cincinnati, a group of veteran officers, was meeting in Philadelphia in May. Washington, who was President of the Society, had told them that he did not want to be reelected, and that he would not be attending—ostensibly because of bad health and the press of private business; in fact, because he wished to avoid controversy over the Society's alleged aristocratic pretensions. (Membership was—and is—hereditary, through firstborn sons.) If, after all that, he showed up in Philadelphia for the convention, wouldn't he be in an "aukward situation"? Nor was his health an empty excuse. Since the fall, he had been suffering from rheumatism "so bad that it is sometimes with difficulty I can raise my hand to my head, or turn myself in bed."[11]

Back of these difficulties and ailments lay a great difficulty (its presence no doubt exacerbating the ailments): the proposed convention was illegal. The Articles of Confederation stipulated that any alteration would require the consent of Congress and of the legislature of every state. Conceivably these fourteen bodies might agree with whatever came out of Philadelphia, but Congress had not yet approved of the meeting, and Rhode Island would not send a delegation. "The legallity of this Convention I do not mean to discuss," wrote Washington to Knox in February. "In strict propriety a Convention so holden may not be legal," he wrote Jay in March. The supporters of the convention were equally aware of the dubious ground on which they stood, which was why they needed Washington to attend. If the hero of the Revolution was among their number, how could they be taxed with impropriety? At the same time, they did not want him to expend his prestige on an enterprise that was unlikely to succeed. "It ought not to be wished by any of his friends," wrote Madison, "that he should participate in any abortive undertaking."[12]

There was also the problem of whether constitutional change was desirable. Much of the political class was happy with the current arrangements: nobly so, to the extent they feared that a strengthened government would encroach on liberty; less nobly, to the extent that they enjoyed being big fish in the small ponds of the states. Supporters of change would have to make the case that a new government would not threaten liberty, and that they were not primarily motivated by the desire to be big fish in the bigger pond of the nation. Washington's presence would help immeasurably to make that case. He had already held more power than any man in America, and after eight and a half years, he had surrendered it. He was the most conspicuous example of moderation and disinterestedness that the nation could supply.

By March, Congress had voted to recommend that the states send delegations to Philadelphia, thus removing one stumbling block, and Washington wrote his governor a sentence whose switchbacks nicely reflect the thought process he had been going through. ". . . I have come to a resolution to go, if my health will permit, provided, from the lapse of time between the date of your Excellency's letter and this reply, the Executive may not, the reverse of which wd. be highly pleasing to me, have turned its thoughts to some other character." "Secure as he was in his fame," wrote Knox to Lafayette, "he has again committed it to the mercy of events."[13] On May 9 the most famous man in America left Mount Vernon. Head- and stomach-aches assailed him as he moved through Maryland, though by the time he reached Philadelphia, he felt well again.

The Convention was scheduled to begin on May 14, but it did not muster a quorum of seven states until the 25th. "These delays," wrote Washington, who showed up on the first day, as he would on every subsequent day, precisely on time, ". . . sour the temper of the punctual members."[14] Fifty-five delegates attended over the course of the summer, though they were never present all at once. Jefferson was in Paris, and John Adams was serving as Minister to London; some other prominent patriots, notably Patrick Henry, the Virginian orator, and John Adams's second cousin Samuel, did not attend because they disapproved of the venture. But eight of the delegates had signed the Declaration of Independence, and twenty-one had fought in the war. For all that, they were a youngish group, with an average age of forty-four. The youngest was only twenty-four; the oldest, Benjamin Franklin, was eighty-one.

Rhode Island never sent a delegation, and most of the New Yorkers left before the New Hampshire delegation arrived, so there were never more than eleven voting delegations at any time. The seven-man Virginia contingent was particularly strong: in addition to Washington and Madison, it included Mason and Edmund Randolph, the governor. Randolph was beholden to Washington: though his father had stayed loyal to the king and gone to England before the war, Washington had put the young man on his staff, which cleared him of any paternal taint. The Virginians were the first out-of-towners to arrive in Philadelphia, and while waiting for a quorum they held daily meetings "in order," as Mason put it delicately, "to form a proper correspondence of sentiments."[15] Like all good politicians, they wanted to set the agenda.

The first order of the convention's business was to elect a president. Franklin was to have nominated Washington for the post. But bad weather kept the old man home, and Robert Morris, the financier and a fellow delegate from Pennsylvania, made the motion in his place. John Rutledge of South Carolina seconded, saying "that the presence of Genl. Washington forbade any observations on the occasion which might otherwise be proper." The constitution makers, and breakers, had their hero, and it was safe to proceed. Morris's motion passed unanimously, and Washington thanked the delegates for the honor, only asking their indulgence for any errors "which his want of experience might occasion."[16]

The most complete set of notes of the Convention was taken by Madison, who wanted the origins of this constitution to be well documented, unlike the origins of all the other constitutions he had studied. Madison drew no portraits of the delegates, however; for that, we must rely on William Pierce of Georgia, who left thumbnail sketches of all of them. Of Madison himself, Pierce wrote: "He always comes forward the best informed Man of any point in debate . . . [f]rom a spirit of industry and application which he possesses in a most eminent degree." He had good and bad to say of Hamilton: "There is no skimming over the surface of a subject with him, he must sink to the bottom to see what foundation it rests on. . . . His manners are tinctured with stiffness, and sometimes with a degree of vanity that is highly disagreeable." Hamilton, in fairness, was in an awkward position: the New York delegation consisted of him and two opponents of the convention. Hamilton did little during the debates, except deliver an elaborate and rather pointless speech on the virtues of monarchies.

Some delegates had been better off unsketched. Richard Bassett (Delaware): "a religious enthusiast, lately turned Methodist . . . has modesty enough to hold his Tongue." Luther Martin (Maryland): "never speaks without tiring the patience of all who hear him." William Houstoun (Georgia): "Nature seems to have done more for his corporeal than mental powers."

Pierce's portraits of Franklin and Washington are more revealing than he realizes.

"Dr. Franklin is well known to be the greatest phylosopher of the present age;—all the operations of nature he seems to understand,—the very heavens obey him, and the Clouds yield up their Lightning to be imprisoned in his rod. But what claim he has to the politician, posterity must determine. It is certain that he does not shine much in public Council,—he is no Speaker, nor does he seem to let politics engage his attention. He is, however, a most extraordinary Man, and tells a story in a style more engaging than anything I ever heard. . . ." Franklin had been in local, national, and international politics for more than fifty years, and he knew his way around at least as well as William Pierce. Pierce does capture the secrets of Franklin's success, however, without knowing that they are political secrets: an impressive reputation outside politics, joined to an unassuming manner and the ability to tell the story that makes the sale, or that makes the person who has already been sold (maybe sold down the river) feel good about it.

"Genl. Washington," wrote Pierce, "is well known. . . . Having conducted these states to independence and peace, he nows appears to assist in framing a Government to make the People happy. Like Gustavus Vasa, he may be said to be the deliverer of his Country;—like Peter the great he appears as the politician and the States-man; and like Cincinnatus he returned to his farm perfectly contented with being only a plain Citizen, after enjoying the highest honor of the Confederacy,—and

now only seeks for the approbation of his Country-men by being virtuous and useful."[17] This seems to tell us almost nothing;
the man disappears behind the record of his deeds and a screen
of heroic names, chosen seemingly at random (many people
compared Washington to Cincinnatus, but the only trait he
shared with Peter the Great was that they were both tall). But
Pierce once again indirectly makes a political point, for his
deeds and his heroism were among the tools that Washington
brought to the work of framing a government.

The esteem in which Washington was held affected his fellow delegates first of all. It was reconfirmed a week into the
Convention, with the first discussion of the executive. Under
the current system, Congress had a President, but he was a presiding officer merely. The plan on the floor proposed to make
the executive a more potent force, and the first motion offered
was to make the executive a single person (it might conceivably
have been a committee). No one rose to address the point.
Madison writes: "A considerable pause ensuing, and the Chairman asking if he should put the question [to a vote], Docr.
Franklin observed that it was a point of great importance and
wished that the gentlemen would deliver their sentiments on it
before the question was put."[18] At that moment, Washington
was not in the chair. The Convention had made itself into a
Committee of the Whole, a procedural device allowing greater
flexibility of discussion, and the chairman of the Committee of
the Whole was Nathaniel Gorham of Massachusetts. But
Washington was in the hall, as a delegate. If there was going to
be a national executive, and if it was going to be one man, he
was the man. A "considerable pause" ensued because, for all the
boldness of the delegates, not one of them seems to have been
bold enough to begin the work of cutting and trimming Washington's next job in his presence. It is significant that the man
to break the logjam was Franklin, the only other delegate with
anything like Washington's prestige.

Pierce provided another example of his, and everyone else's, awe of Washington when some delegate dropped a copy of proposed resolutions in the State House, where the Convention was meeting. At the end of the day's business, "the General arose from his seat. . . . 'I must entreat Gentlemen to be more careful, least our transactions get into the News Papers, and disturb the public repose by premature speculations. I know not whose Paper it is, but there it is (throwing it down on the table), let him who owns it take it.' At the same time he bowed, picked up his Hat, and quitted the room with a dignity so severe that every Person seemed alarmed; for my part I was extremely so, for putting my hand in my pocket I missed my copy of the same Paper. . . ." Back in his room, Pierce was relieved to find his copy in a coat pocket. He adds, "It is something remarkable that no Person ever owned the Paper."[19]

Washington did not wield the power he possessed by speaking. Apart from his lecture on secrecy, he did not address the Convention between the first day and the last. Biographers desperate for grist about his role speculate about who he may have talked to after hours (Washington's diaries are laconic, mostly being a record of where he ate) or grasp at even slighter straws. Almost forty years after the Convention, a friend of one of the delegates, Jonathan Dayton of New Jersey, wrote an elaborate account of Washington's changing facial expressions in the chair. During a deadlock in the discussions, Franklin had proposed that the Convention engage a chaplain to open its meetings with prayer. "*God governs in the affairs of men,*" the old politician said. "And if a sparrow cannot fall to the ground without his notice, is it possible that an empire can rise without his aid?" Dayton's friend described Washington following the debate: "The bosom of Washington seemed to labor with the most anxious solicitude. . . . Here the countenance of Washington brightened. . . . Washington fixed his eye upon the speaker with a mixture of *surprise* and *indignation.* . . ."

The story is quite unreliable, since Dayton's amaneunsis asserts that Franklin's motion passed, whereas in fact it died without being brought to a vote. Evidently most of the delegates agreed with Hamilton, at whom Washington was supposed to have looked indignantly, who argued that hiring a chaplain in midstream would look desperate. (It is always worse to look desperate than to be desperate.) Hugh Williamson of North Carolina ("no Orator," wrote Pierce) also pointed out that the convention had no funds.[20]

Washington's most substantive contribution to the Convention was not his words or his frowns, but his endorsement of the plan that became the basis for its discussions. This was what the Virginians had been working on when they arrived in Philadelphia early, and indeed the process of drafting it had been set in motion months before. At the end of March, as Washington's thoughts began to incline toward attending, he wrote Madison a letter in which he said he hoped that the Convention would address itself to "radical cures. . . . This will require thought." As luck would have it, Madison had been thinking; he had already sent a plan for a new constitution to Jefferson. Madison wrote back to Washington agreeing that "radical attempts" were necessary and that he had "*some* outlines of a new system," which he took "the liberty of submitting . . . to your eye."[21] Washington, as was his wont, made a digest of it before leaving Mount Vernon.

The Virginia plan, as Madison's proposal became known, was read on the third day of the Convention by Randolph. Washington had written Madison that he hoped the convention would produce a "Congress [which] will upon all proper occasions exercise the powers with a firm and steady hand, instead of frittering them back to the Individual States where the members in place of viewing themselves in their National character, are too apt to be looking." The Virginia plan certainly did that. It called, as Washington's summary of Madison's draft put it, for a "due supremacy of the national authority," including "local authorities [only] whenever they can be subordinately useful." Its most striking feature was a proposal that the Congress have the power to veto any state law it considered unconstitutional. Madison had originally called for an even more sweeping national power over state laws—a "negative *in all cases* whatever." When Randolph was done, Charles Pinckney of South Carolina asked, not unreasonably, "whether he meant to abolish the State Governts. altogether."[22]

The states that felt they had the most to lose under such a consolidated system counterattacked two and a half weeks later with a plan read by William Paterson of New Jersey, which was essentially the current system with additional powers, most importantly the power to tax. For the cautious, the New Jersey plan had the advantage of being less of a change. For the scrupulous, it had the advantage of conforming to the instructions with which many of the delegations had been saddled by the state legislatures that sent them, allowing them only to propose amendments to the existing constitution. For the rest of June, and on into July, the two sides wrangled. The most prominent supporters of the Virginia plan did little to allay the fears of the partisans of states' rights. Hamilton remarked at one point that the state governments "might gradually dwindle into nothing." Madison managed to be equally tactless, supposing "for a moment" that the states should be "reduced to corporations. . . . Why shd. it follow that the Genl. Govt. wd. take from the states any branch of their power as far as it was beneficial?" But the most offensive comment was delivered by Gouverneur Morris of Pennsylvania ("No Man has more wit," wrote Pierce, "nor can any one engage the attention more than Mr. Morris. . . . But with all these powers he is fickle and inconstant"): "This Country must be united," said Morris. "If persuasion does not unite it, the sword will." This prompted Paterson to observe that talk of swords was "little calculated to produce conviction."[23]

Washington avoided the possibility of provocative remarks by keeping silent. But he was also able to show a spirit of moderation in a few of the votes he cast as a delegate. Early in June, there was a vote on broadening the congress's power to veto state laws from cases where it judged them to be unconstitutional, to all cases (Madison's original plan). Virginia supported the motion, Madison notes, by a vote of three to two. He adds, oddly, that "Genl. W." was "not consulted."[24] How could he not have been consulted? He never missed a session. Most probably, Genl. W. had been consulted privately, and the result of the consultation was that, since Madison had the votes anyway, Washington chose not to take a public stand on an inflamed issue.

Two months later, Madison was hotly resisting a motion to restrict the power of originating money bills to the lower house of the new Congress. Many state constitutions included such a restriction, but Madison wanted both houses of the national legislature to have as much freedom of action as possible. His tightly argued and urgent reasoning drew a notable rebuke from John Dickinson of Delaware. "Reason may mislead us. It was not Reason that discovered the singular & admirable mechanism of the English Constitution. It was not Reason that discovered or ever could have discovered the odd . . . mode of trial by Jury. Accidents probably produced these discoveries, and experience has given a sanction to them. This is then our guide." On this occasion, Virginia voted against Madison and for experience, three to two, and Washington went with the majority. Madison wrote that though Washington had until then voted the other way, "he gave up his judgment" because the matter "was not of very material weight with him & was made an essential point with others who if disappointed, might be less cordial in other points of real weight."[25] Madison's use of the word "cordial" suggests that Washington's behavior and the behavior he sought to elicit from the delegates he disagreed with was a matter of manners or mere politeness. But real politeness is always something more than "mere." It acknowledges the importance of someone else's rights and point of view. Similarly, moderation can represent more than indifference, impotence, or weakness of mind. It can signify the desire to bring others along, because you need or respect them, instead of ramming something down their throats. Washington's moderation and political cordiality were his final service to the Convention.

To note that Madison and his allies acted differently than Washington is not to belittle either course of action. Madison and his soulmates were intellectuals, enamored of their ideas; they were young politicians, engaged in trench warfare. They were also, at the end of the day, pragmatic enough to give ground when they were beaten. Because of his relative age (fifty-five), his experience, and his prominence, Washington could afford to hang back and let himself be guided by different principles. Almost a century later, a descendant of Oliver Ellsworth, a Connecticut delegate, reported a family tradition that "Judge Ellsworth" had once said, "Washington's influence while in the Convention was not very great . . ." (Ellsworth added, with pride and some accuracy, that the prime movers had been Madison and five others, including himself). Certainly as far as words uttered or arguments made, Ellsworth was right. But arguments are not won only by arguing, and words do not always have the last word. Two months after the Convention adjourned, Washington summarized his notions of the proper style of legislative leadership in a letter to a nephew, who had just entered the Virginia assembly. "Speak seldom. . . . Never exceed a *decent* warmth, and submit your sentiments with diffidence. A dictatorial Stile, though it may carry conviction, is always accompanied with disgust." (Shortly thereafter, he wrote a friend that he hoped his nephew would not "become a babbler.") Years later, Jefferson, recalling that he had served with Washington in the House of Burgesses and with Franklin in Congress, wrote that "I never heard either of them speak ten minutes at a time, nor to any but the main point. . . . They laid their shoulders to the great points, knowing that the little ones would follow of themselves."[26]

In the course of threats and counterthreats and conciliation, much of the Virginia plan was heavily altered. Every state, large and small, got equal representation in the Senate; Congress's veto on state laws disappeared entirely. But the great point established by the Virginia plan was that the Convention would devote itself to "radical cures." Some of the Virginia plan's enemies opposed radical cures altogether. Hamilton's fellow delegates from New York left Philadelphia in disgust early in July, and the long-winded Luther Martin followed in August. But most of the backers of the New Jersey plan wanted serious reform, so long as their states were not thrown into a "hotchpot."[27]

As the Convention wound up its work in mid-September, however, three of the delegates who remained decided that they could not sign. Two of them were Virginians. Edmund Randolph, who had given the Convention's first significant speech, now showed a hesitancy that would serve him ill in later years. The other Virginia holdout was George Mason, who had come to fear "the dangerous power and structure of the Government, concluding that it would end either in monarchy, or a tyrannical aristocracy; which, he was in doubt, but one or the other, he was sure." The Constitution, Mason went on, "had been formed without the knowledge or idea of the people." This was true enough. Only if a second convention, giving an opportunity for comment and amendments, were called could Mason sign.

Charles Pinckney rose to rebut. Such "declarations from members so respectable" gave "a peculiar solemnity to the present moment." He "descanted" on the "confusion and contrariety" that another convention would produce. He had his own objections to the Constitution, but "the danger of a general confusion, and an ultimate decision by the sword" made him willing to sign it. A motion for a second convention failed, but the feeling of "peculiar solemnity" lingered.[28]

Here was the last great point, and on the last day of the Convention, Franklin and Washington both put their shoulders to it. Randolph, Mason, and Pinckney had spoken on a Saturday, and between then and Monday, Franklin prepared a speech which, as with the nomination of Washington, was read for him. As always, he had an engaging story, whose punchline he attributed to a "french lady": "I don't know how it happens, Sister, but I meet with no body but myself, that's always in the right—*Il n'y a que moi qui a toujours raison.*" But he began with a considerable piece of wisdom. ". . . having lived long, I have experienced many instances of being obliged by better information, or fuller consideration, to change opinions even on important subjects, which I once thought right, but found to be otherwise. It is therefore that the older I grow, the more apt I am to doubt my own judgment, and to pay more respect to the judgment of others." He ended by wishing "that every member of the Convention who may still have objections to it, would with me, on this occasion doubt a little of his own infallibility. . . ." And then, politician to the last, he slipped in a ruse, suggested by Gouverneur Morris: since the state delegations had approved the Constitution unanimously, all the delegates could sign "In Witness" to the fact.

Washington's approach was more oblique. After Franklin

finished, Nathaniel Gorham offered a last-minute amendment, to shrink the size of a representative's constituency from forty to thirty thousand. This was a matter which had been debated, and settled, a month earlier. Now Washington rose to agree with Gorham. His "situation," he explained, "had hitherto restrained him from offering his sentiments on questions depending in the House, and it might be thought, ought now to impose silence on him." Yet "it was much to be desired that the objections to the plan recommended might be made as few as possible." The large size of districts had always struck him as "exceptionable," and "late as the present moment was for admitting amendments, he thought this of so much consequence that it would give much satisfaction to see it adopted."[29] Historians debate the motive for Washington's appeal. Some see it as a sign of his commitment to localism and government by neighborhoods. Others see it in the same light as his vote on the appropriations question—a tactical retreat by a supporter of a smaller, and therefore more vigorous, legislature, willing to sacrifice that goal in the interest of harmony. Maybe it is best to see it as a seal of approval. The size of districts was not a major issue. By breaking his silence to endorse a minor change, Washington was signifying to the delegates that no major changes needed to be made. The additional fact that the gesture expressed diffidence toward Gorham and those who had seconded his motion would have made it all the more characteristic of him. Without further discussion, Gorham's amendment passed unanimously.

At the end of the day, the dissenters were unmoved by the wisdom, the ruse, the approval, or the diffidence. There was no unanimity, no final burst of feel-good togetherness. Thirty-eight of the forty-one delegates remaining in Philadelphia signed (John Dickinson's signature was affixed by a colleague). Washington would be reconciled with Randolph, thereby preparing difficulties for both of them. His friendship with Mason, his old advisor, was permanently ruptured. But Franklin and Washington, who had started the Convention off, had sent its handiwork into the world.

The debates at the Convention, however important to the delegates and interesting to us, were secret: Madison's notes were not published until 1840. The public debate took place in the ratifying conventions of the states and in newspapers and pamphlets. The active roles in this struggle were filled, as at the Convention, by younger men, most notably Madison and Hamilton, who stage-managed the fights in their respective states and, in their spare time, wrote eighty-five articles, with some help from John Jay, known as *The Federalist Papers*. One of Hamilton's subtlest arguments was against a Bill of Rights, an addition to the Constitution urged by critics such as Mason: the very enumeration of fundamental rights, Hamilton wrote, would tempt the government to stretch itself. It "would contain various exceptions to powers which are not granted; and, on this very account, would afford a colorable pretext to claim more than were granted. For why declare that things shall not be done which there is no power to do?"[30] The argument was a nonstarter. In several states the Constitution passed with the understanding that a Bill of Rights would be among the first order of the new government's business.

Washington's role, though large, was largely implicit. From the fall of 1787 to the summer of 1788, he read everything that he could buy on the controversy, pro and con. He arranged for *The Federalist Papers* to be reprinted in Richmond, to help the Constitution in Virginia, and after the battle was over, he gave Hamilton what would today be thought of as a handsome blurb: "When the transient circumstances and fugitive performances which attended this Crisis shall have disappeared, That

Work will merit the Notice of Posterity." He told Madison to use his name in letters, and in April 1788, when it looked as if Maryland's convention might adjourn without ratifying, thus setting back the cause in Virginia, where it was still up in the air, he wrote Thomas Johnson, a former governor, who also happened to be an old friend, urging him to keep the Marylanders in session. He also told Johnson that he hoped he had not exceeded "the proper limit" in doing so.[31]

Washington also figured as a subject of debate. The Constitution's enemies had to clamber over the fact of his endorsement, as best they might. "The name of Washington," Luther Martin assured the convention in Maryland, "is far above my praise"—a sure sign that praise was coming anyway, which it promptly did. "I would to Heaven that on this occasion one more wreath had been added to the number of those which are twined around his amiable brow—that those with which it is already surrounded may flourish with immortal verdure, nor wither or fade till time shall be no more, is my fervent prayer, and may that glory which encircles his head ever shine with undiminished rays."[32] The purpose of these laborious tributes was not to add to Washington's reputation, but to protect Martin's; only after they were in place could he resume his assaults.

Interestingly, even a supporter of the Constitution expressed a private doubt about the effects of Washington's prestige. "Entre Nous," wrote Pierce Butler of South Carolina to his brother, the powers of the presidency had been made too great because they had been apportioned with Washington's character in mind. "So that the Man, who by his Patriotism and Virtue, Contributed largely to the Emancipation of his Country, may be the Innocent means of its being, when He is lay'd low, oppress'd."[33]

Such worries concerned the future. For now, no one doubted that the new office was to be occupied by the man who had presided over the creation of it and the rest of the system. His silent presence affected the debate like an eighty-sixth *Federalist Paper*. "Be assured," James Monroe, an opponent of the Constitution, wrote Jefferson, "his influence carried this government."[34]

Washington's evident destiny as the first president, though it helped ensure a goal he desired, filled him with anxiety. In the fall of 1788, he wrote Hamilton that he felt "a kind of gloom" upon his mind. By the following spring, he was writing Henry Knox that his "movements to the chair of government" would be "accompanied by feelings not unlike those of a culprit who is going to the place of his execution." On occasion, he suggested that destiny might pass him by: there could be opposition to him in the Electoral College, or "some other person" might be found who "could execute all the duties full as satisfactorily as myself."[35]

Some of this should not be taken seriously. No one equaled Washington in popular esteem, and no politician, whatever he thought of the Constitution, would oppose him personally. Washington surely knew that he would be elected, and that if elected, he would serve. But that does not mean that his fears and his worries were unreal or unfounded.

One category of anxieties concerned his reputation—for competence and, especially, for good character. Washington had risked both greatly during the war (if he had lost, he and not Arnold would have been known to history as a traitor). If, as Knox had written Lafayette, Washington had risked his reputation again in going to the Convention, how much more would he risk it in taking public office? Before he even took office, did not the very act of coming out of retirement leave him open to the charge of "*inconsistency* and *ambition*"? The concern for reputation led Washington into finer scruples than this. Even to ask whether or not he might be elected "might be construed into a vain-glorious desire of pushing myself into notice as a candidate."[36]

Washington was even more anxious for the reputation of the principle of self-government, which he believed was linked to the fate of the American government. He was not alone in thinking so. At moments, during the months in Philadelphia, the hot room containing forty-some politicians disputing the legal arrangements of less than three million people in the eighteenth-century equivalent of the Third World fell away to reveal larger vistas. Hamilton, who signed the Constitution, said that if the Convention failed, "Republican Government" would be "disgraced & lost to mankind forever." Elbridge Gerry of Massachusetts, who did not sign the Constitution, said that if they failed, "we would disappoint not only America, but the whole world." Maybe only men who were simultaneously so intelligent and so provincial would have been naïve enough to believe and noble enough to hope that their deliberations might have such significance. Washington shared the belief and the hope. "It has always been my creed," he wrote to Lafayette, "that we should not be left as an awful monument to prove, 'that Mankind, under the most favourable circumstances for civil liberty and happiness, are unequal to the task of Governing themselves, and therefore made for a Master.' "[37] The first system of government of the United States had failed; the Constitution was an attempt, maybe the last, at a "more perfect union." Once he became President, no one would have more responsibility than Washington to see that it succeeded.

The old Congress fixed the first Wednesday in January 1789 as the date for choosing presidential electors. On the first Wednesday in February they were to meet in their respective states and cast their ballots. Today each elector votes for president and for vice-president. Then, and until the election of 1800, each elector cast two votes, without reference to an office: the candidate with the most votes would become president, while the candidate with the second-highest total would become vice-president. On the first Wednesday in March, the new Congress was to convene in New York, the capital, and count the ballots, but the new body did not assemble a quorum until the end of the month. On April 14, the Secretary of Congress arrived at Mount Vernon to tell Washington that every elector had cast a vote for him—in other words, his election was unanimous—and that the President pro tempore of the Senate "indulge[d] the hope that so auspicious a mark of public confidence will meet your approbation."[38]

Washington's journey north was an almost uninterrupted series of banquets, speeches, toasts, parades, and all the other ceremonies that a small country could devise. In Philadelphia, twenty thousand people turned out to cheer him along; the population of the city was twenty-eight thousand. In Trenton, he was greeted by a rudimentary form of theater. At the bridge over Assunpink Creek stood an arch of evergreens and flowers and a "numerous train" of women and girls in white robes. On the arch hung a banner: THE DEFENDER OF THE MOTHERS WILL BE THE PROTECTOR OF THE DAUGHTERS. Twelve years earlier, Washington and his "noble horse" had stood on the bridge, "firm, composed, and majestic," giving confidence to retreating soldiers. Then it had been a scene of darkness, men, and death. Now it was a scene of light, women, and peace. The state begins in violence, but unless it ends in freedom and order it is brigandage. Thirteen girls, with baskets of flowers, sang him a song.

> Virgins fair and matrons grave,
> Those thy conquering arms did save,
> Build for thee triumphant bowers.
> Strew, ye fair, his way with flowers—
> Strew your hero's way with flowers.[39]

PRESIDENT

The celebrations continued all the way to New York. Washington made the last leg of the journey, across the harbor from New Jersey, on a ceremonial barge, manned by thirteen oarsmen—a hopeful number, since North Carolina and Rhode Island had not yet ratified. A Spanish frigate saluted it with guns larger than any the United States possessed; porpoises frolicked alongside. Washington landed at the bottom of Wall Street and walked, through dense, cheering crowds, to a rented house.

The adulatory welcome, Washington wrote in his diary, "filled my mind with sensations as painful . . . as they were pleasing," because he found himself "contemplating the reverse of this scene," which might come about even "after all my efforts to do good." He was still solemn a week later, when he was inaugurated at the original Federal Hall. One senator described him as "grave, almost to sadness," another as "agitated and embarrassed." Washington had written a long address, surprisingly personal in places, of which only fragments survive (a nineteenth-century historian cut it up for handwriting samples). Madison persuaded Washington to give a short speech instead, in which he told his listeners that "the destiny of the republican model of government" was "staked on the experiment entrusted to the[ir] hands." His earnest performance, wrote a congressman, "seemed to me an allegory in which virtue was personified and addressing those whom she would make her votaries."[1]

The first important task facing virtue's votaries was to develop an etiquette appropriate to the republican model of government. The task fell most heavily on the President because, while Congress had existed in one form or another since 1774, the presidency was new. Washington had to decide how to behave toward others and how others should behave toward him, without precedents to guide him. The new Congress had settled his title the week before his inauguration. The Senate wanted something sonorous—Oliver Ellsworth noted that even "fire companies" and "cricket club[s]" had presidents[2]— but the House insisted on "President of the United States."

During his stay in New York, and after the capital moved to Philadelphia in August 1790, he lived in rented houses, which he had to make suitable for entertaining. Two months after his inauguration, he asked his secretary to buy a set of "waiters, salvers, or whatever they are called," meaning table ornaments, but since nothing satisfactory could be found in America, Gouverneur Morris went shopping in Paris. He bought twelve porcelain allegories of the arts and sciences, with a centerpiece depicting "Apollo Instructing the Shepherds," and wrote Washington that his purchases were "of a noble Simplicity. . . . I think it of very great importance to fix the taste of our Country properly. . . . It is therefore my Wish that every Thing about you should be substantially good and majestically plain. . . ."

Despite these adornments, the French minister found Washington's New York residence *chetive* (mean), while his mode of living struck the secretary of the Dutch legation as "frugal."[3]

Apart from formal dinners, Washington had to cope with a flood of callers even greater than that which had deluged him in Mount Vernon. During his first days in office, he wrote to a friend in Virginia, "I was unable to attend to any business whatsoever, for gentlemen, consulting their own convenience rather than mine, were calling from the time I rose for breakfast—often before—until I sat down to dinner." Washington's solution was to hold a reception from three to four on Tuesday afternoons, for anyone who chose to come. He tried to strike a balance between ceremony and informality. When an eager aide announced Washington's entrance at a reception by crying, "The President of the United States!" Washington rebuked him: "You have taken me in once, but by God, you shall never take me in a second time." Thereafter, Washington was to be found posted in the reception room in formal dress—black coat and dress sword in a white leather scabbard—as the callers arrived. "Gentlemen," he wrote, "often in great numbers, come and go, chat with each other, and act as they please. A porter shows them into the room, and they retire from it when they choose. . . . What pomp there is in all this I am unable to discover." Visitors with experience of European manners agreed with him. When the painter Gilbert Stuart, who had lived in London for thirteen years, came to one of the receptions in Philadelphia, he assumed that he was in an antechamber, awaiting some formal ceremony of presentation, and was startled when the President came over and introduced himself. But others had no trouble discovering the pomp. The very idea of public appearances at stated times reminded Senator William Maclay, an early populist from Pennsylvania, of "an Eastern lama."[4]

He also had political precedents to establish. The Constitution gives the President the power to make treaties "with the Advice and Consent" of the Senate, so before sending negotiators to the Creek Indians, Washington went to the Senate to get its advice. As the Vice-President read the proposed terms, "carriages were driving past," wrote Senator Maclay, "and such a noise! I could tell it was something about Indians, but was not master of one sentence of it." After closing the windows, the Senate began an inconclusive discussion and finally asked to see papers. "*This defeats every purpose of my coming here!*" Washington exclaimed, in what Maclay called a "violent fret." The Creeks were postponed to another day. When the President returned to the Senate, he was "placid and serene," but he was also overheard to say, after the business had been concluded, that he would "be damned if he ever went there again" for such a purpose.[5] No president has.

On most other occasions, social and political, Washington blended amiability and reserve. In 1792, he wrote a letter of advice to Gouverneur Morris, much like the one he had written to his nephew five years earlier. Morris had just been confirmed as minister to France, but Washington wanted him to know that Morris's opponents in the Senate had accused him of "imprudence of conversation and conduct. It was urged that your habits of expression indicated a *hauteur* disgusting to those who happen to differ from you in sentiment." Morris was thought to be prone to "sallies which too often offend" and "ridicule . . . which begets enmity." Both might be avoided if his "lively and brilliant imagination" were "under the control of more caution and prudence." This was good advice for Morris; it was also an exposition of Washington's own ideal of public behavior. "His eyes retire inward (do you understand me?)," wrote the secretary of a British diplomat, "and have nothing of fire or animation or openness in their expression. If this circumspection is accompanied by discernment and penetration, as I am informed it is . . . he possesses the two great requisites of a statesman, the faculty of concealing his own sentiments and of discovering those of other men." He "possessed the gift of silence," recalled John Adams, years later.[6]

The need for silence was all the greater in Washington's case because he was a very great man, living in a very small country. Washington was a world figure and, for all that Americans spoke of the United States as a "rising empire," it was tiny by European standards. The small-time quality of America asserts itself again and again in the details of the Washington administration. When Washington toured the country, he employed no advance men. The President and his companions often arrived at inns unannounced. When he visited New England, the wife of one innkeeper sent them away, since her husband wasn't there to admit them. On a tour of the South, the president's party breakfasted at an inn that had unusually good food and service, only to discover, at meal's end, that they had unwittingly intruded upon a private house. When the federal government was in New York, Madison, who had entered the House of Representatives, lived in a boarding house and Jefferson, the Secretary of State, put up at a tavern. John Adams, who had been elected Vice-President, had to find a house in the country, in Greenwich Village. When the government evacuated Philadelphia during a yellow fever epidemic, Jefferson could not even find a room to himself, but had to sleep in a corner of the public room of an inn.

The new government had other shortcomings besides logistics. In 1795, Thomas Pinckney was sent to Madrid to negotiate an important treaty with Spain. In the end, he got a good treaty, though it was hard to tell back in Philadelphia how the negotiations were going, since Pinckney's dispatches were written in a cipher that no one at the State Department could decode. More people, indeed, worked at Mount Vernon than in the entire executive branch of the federal government. And yet a visiting English architect described Mount Vernon as a "plain English country gentleman's home of five or six hundred pounds a year." George Custis, Washington's stepgrandson, remembered one dinner at the country gentleman's home that never got served because a hound stole the ham out of the kitchen. There was a simplicity to American manners that could seem dull or boorish: one wintry Tuesday afternoon in New York, when Congress was out of session, Washington dressed and positioned himself for his reception—and nobody showed up. Yet when Americans wanted to put on a show, they did it with excesses of provincial enthusiasm: at a concert in the President's honor in Charleston, the ladies wore bandeux on their foreheads bearing mottoes such as "Health to Columbia's noblest son/ Her light, her shield—great Washington."[7] During the war, Washington had compared the mechanism of government to a clock. The clock of the United States was intricate and in some ways beautiful. But it was small and fragile: a miniature. Carelessness on his part might easily wreck it.

The little country had one thing in plentiful supply: political energy. It is a truism that the Framers did not envision political parties, and it is true that they did not write them into the Constitution. But within five years after the Constitution was written, the very same Framers had created a rudimentary party system: Federalists around Treasury Secretary Hamilton, Republicans around Madison (and Jefferson).

For the first year and a half, everyone had pulled together. The great policy achievement of this spell of good feeling was a bargain struck in 1790 whereby the southern states, particularly Virginia, agreed to let the federal government assume state debts (mostly northern) that were still outstanding from the Revolution; in return, the northerners agreed to fix the eventual site of the capital on the Potomac, bypassing New York and Philadelphia. The final deal was made one night in June when Jefferson had Hamilton and Madison to dinner. Washington heartily approved both halves of their bargain, for his experience as Commander in Chief had made him a confirmed foe of weak credit, and a capital city on the Potomac would be a boost to the trans-Appalachian canal (if it ever got dug), besides being convenient to his house. The leaders got along personally as well as politically. That summer Washington took Hamilton and Jefferson on a three-day fishing trip off Sandy Hook.

But the bargain carried the seeds of later conflict. The new financial arrangements led to a burst of speculative investment in government securities, which Hamilton had foreseen and desired. Madison and Jefferson, who had not foreseen it, were appalled. The Treasury Secretary, who had grown up working in a merchant house in St. Croix, envisioned the United States as a bustling commercial empire. The Virginians, especially Jefferson, wanted an agricultural republic, essentially a big Virginia, or the Virginia of their dreams. Temperamental differences exacerbated their disagreements. Hamilton was a know-it-all, who (even worse) often did know it all. Madison, beneath a layer of intense shyness, was equally headstrong, while Jefferson had the deep deviousness that is given only to the pure of heart. Hamilton abused his new enemies in anonymous essays in the papers; Jefferson, who was too cagey to write anything for publication himself, kept a journalistic hatchet-man on the State Department payroll. When Jefferson left the cabinet in 1793, and Hamilton in 1795, their opposition continued.

The young stars of the Washington administration, in the cabinet and out of it, were not unusual in their animosities. Politically, the 1790s and the first years of the nineteenth century was an unusually turbulent period—the historian Marshall Smelser called it "the Age of Passion."[8] Americans were passionate because the stakes were so high. So much was being decided for the first time, and it seemed as if anything, once settled, might be decided for the last time. During the Washington administration, a Secretary of State was forced to resign under suspicion of treason; other members of the cabinet carried on private dealings with foreign diplomats which failed to disgrace them only because they remained unknown. A congressional leader was stabbed in a political argument. The year Washington retired from office, the Senate expelled a Senator for treason, and a Republican journalist accused Hamilton of scheming with James Reynolds, a small-time criminal, to speculate in Treasury certificates. Hamilton replied that the only reason he knew Reynolds was because Reynolds had been blackmailing him for having an affair with his wife. A duel between Hamilton and Senator James Monroe, who had leaked the tale, was only averted by Aaron Burr. A year after that, two congressmen fought on the floor of the House. The election of 1800 was the most scurrilous in American history. In 1802 Hamilton's journalistic nemesis, who had switched sides, accused Jefferson of having an affair with his slave Sally Hemings. Hamilton, who had been losing political duels for years, finally lost a real one, to Burr, in 1804.

The American Age of Passion coincided with, and was partly exacerbated by, the beginning of the Age of Ideology in Europe. Three months after Washington's inauguration, the Bastille was stormed. Lafayette sent Washington the key, as "a tribute" from "a missionary of liberty to its patriarch"; Washington hung it proudly in a case in the presidential residence. Both men, at the dawn of the French Revolution, saw it as a parallel and an extension of their own achievements in America. They were wrong. Washington came to suspect it; in June

1792, he wrote Lafayette that "the just medium" between oppression and license "cannot . . . be found in a moment."[9] Two months later, Lafayette's fellow revolutionaries condemned him as a traitor and forced him into exile. The French Revolution, and the reaction to it, inaugurated a quarter century of world wars and rewrote the political discourse of the Western world. America's revolutionaries had operated from different premises and thought in different terms. They got in just under the wire. Still, the effects of the upheaval were felt here, as domestic brawls were carried on in the alien idioms of revolutionary and counterrevolutionary Europe. The fallout from the European struggle was not only rhetorical. France and England had been fighting each other in North America for over a century, and neither country had outgrown the habit of trying to pull the continent into its orbit.

Washington was distressed by the contentions arising in his official family, and he often wished, almost naïvely, that they would go away. "My earnest wish and my fondest hope therefore," he wrote plaintively at one point to Jefferson, "is that, instead of wounding suspicions and irritable charges, there may be liberal allowances, mutual forbearances, and temporizing yieldings on *all sides.*" (Jefferson's answer characterized Hamilton as "a man whose history, from the moment at which history can stoop to notice him, is a tissue of machinations against the liberty of the country. . . .")[10] Washington resisted the tug of domestic politics not only from wishful thinking, but from policy. His wishes flowed from his policy. American passions, homegrown and imported, might well have swept the country apart. If Washington had partaken of them, they certainly would have. But Washington's policy was not one of neutrality at all costs or of doing nothing. The caretakers of the "republican model of government" had to demonstrate that it could govern. When it was not necessary that he act, then it was necessary that he not act. But when the power to govern itself was challenged, then action on his part was required.

The two most serious challenges to self-government, the Whiskey Rebellion and the fight over Jay's Treaty, arose in Washington's second term.

Washington's inclination was not to have a second term. In May of 1792, complaining of the "fatigues and disagreeableness" of office, he asked Madison to prepare a farewell address. Madison sent him a draft, but added that, though he had "complied with your wishes," his own were that Washington would make "one more sacrifice . . . to the desire & interests of your country." Hamilton and Jefferson stopped quarreling long enough to beg him to stay on. Hamilton echoed Madison, urging Washington to a "further sacrifice." The man who had coined the phrase "pursuit of happiness" now told Washington that there were some characters of such "eminence" that society might justly "controul" their pursuit of it, by demanding their services.[11]

One of Washington's nonpolitical associates took a different, and perhaps more effective, tack. Eliza Powel was the wife of a rich Philadelphia merchant; Abigail Adams, who was not easily impressed, judged her "very interesting." Mrs. Powel had known Washington since the war, and in November she added her voice to those of the politicians. She too spoke the language of sacrifice: ". . . you have frequently demonstrated that you possess an empire over yourself. For God's sake, do not yield that empire to a love of ease." But she also appealed, with considerable subtlety, to his concern for his reputation. If he stepped down now, "the envious and malignant" would say that he had left "a station that promised nothing [more] to your ambition and that might eventually involve your popularity."[12] They would say, in other words, that he had been *too con-*

cerned with his reputation. Certainly a man as concerned as Washington was could not permit that.

Whatever his private reluctance, Washington made no public move to refuse reelection. When the electoral votes were counted in February 1793, the tally for him was once again unanimous.

The first great crisis of his second term had its roots in the grand financial bargain of the first. There had been partisan strife over Hamilton's financial policy ever since Madison and Jefferson realized what it entailed. But this was only a battle of words and ideas. By 1794, another aspect of the new fiscal order threatened real battles throughout the Appalachian backcountry between the government and the "hardy race" whose loyalty Washington had worried about when he was planning canals a decade earlier.

The government needed a source of revenue if it was to pay off its debts and the debts of the states which it had assumed. The source to which it turned was an excise on whiskey. Excises were a form of taxation that was particularly disliked: Johnson's *Dictionary* had defined "excise" as "a hateful tax on commodities." Yet there was no alternative. Madison admitted that imports—the source he and Hamilton had looked to as young congressmen ten years earlier—were "already loaded as far as they will bear." An income tax was, of course, unconstitutional. Of all the articles that might be taxed, "distilled spirits are the least objectionable."[13] In theory, the whiskey tax fell most heavily on the farmers of the frontier, for whom whiskey was both the drink of choice and the most convenient form in which to bring a grain crop to market. In practice, few of them paid it. Tax collectors were tarred and feathered, when they dared to venture into the backcountry at all.

The federal government focused its efforts to increase compliance on western Pennsylvania, not because it was the wildest part of the frontier, but because it seemed to be the tamest. Pittsburgh, which had been the object of frontier warfare in the 1750s, was now a flourishing settlement. John Nevile, a rich local landowner and distiller who had opposed the tax when it was first passed, agreed to become an Inspector of Excise responsible for collecting it. Nevile's switch and his stiff neck, however, made him unpopular. His exertions met with little success and came to an abrupt end in the middle of July 1794 when five hundred local militiamen surrounded his estate outside Pittsburgh, traded shots with his slaves and a platoon of soldiers protecting him, and finally burned his house down. Two or three militiamen had been killed, including their commander, a Revolutionary War veteran, and one of the soldiers may have been mortally wounded.

The clash inflamed the situation. Local leaders who deplored violence even though they had opposed the tax now tried to cool down their neighbors, without becoming targets themselves. One politician, Hugh Henry Brackenridge, attended a meeting which debated whether to elect him governor of a new state or to burn his house. He managed to avoid both fates. On August 1, seven thousand rebels met in Braddock's Field outside Pittsburgh—where Washington had fought almost forty years earlier—to overawe the town, or perhaps to overrun it. They raised a flag with six stripes, representing four counties in Pennsylvania and two in Virginia. "Sodom had been burnt by fire from heaven," one speaker said; "this second Sodom [Pittsburgh] should be burned with fire from earth." "I have a bad hat now," another rebel declared, displaying it, "but I expect to get a better one soon." A man with a tomahawk rode into town chanting, "A great deal more is to be done; I am but beginning yet." The town was neither burned nor plundered, in part because the residents treated the rebels to free whiskey. But many feared, or hoped, that the horseman would make good on his threat, with the help of his fellows. Brackenridge wrote to the capital that "should an attempt be made to suppress these people, I am afraid the question will not be, whether you will march to Pittsburgh, but whether they will march to Philadelphia. . . ."[14] Western Pennsylvania was not the only locus of unrest; altogether there were disturbances in twenty frontier counties—four of them, ironically, named after Washington.

The namesake of the rebellious counties had now to decide what to do. The advice he was given covered a range of options. Secretary of the Treasury Hamilton, whose policies were the occasion for the unrest, wanted to call out the militia to restore order. ". . . the very existence of Government," he told the president, "demands this course. . . ." Secretary of War Henry Knox, who eight years earlier had kept Washington informed (and misinformed) about Shays' Rebellion, also called for action. William Bradford, the Attorney General, agreed that a show of force was necessary, but urged that it not be made until "the public mind [was] satisfied that all other means in the power of the Executive have failed. . . ." Edmund Randolph, who had replaced Jefferson as Secretary of State, wanted Washington to send out a commission to study the situation, in the interests of "humanity" and "conciliation." The Governor of Pennsylvania met with the cabinet and told them that he doubted whether the state militia would answer his call, so generally was the excise disliked. Early in August, Washington chose from this array of advice a double-tracked response. He ordered Knox to prepare a force of over twelve thousand men, drawn from the four states closest to the outbreak. He also sent three commissioners to western Pennsylvania, including the Attorney General. Washington, wrote Bradford, was seeking "to convince these people and the world of the *moderation & the firmness*" of the government: a show of mildness, and a show of force.[15]

Meanwhile, the rebels had become confused. Beyond refusing to pay the tax, it was not clear what they were willing to do. At the end of August, a committee of sixty met to consider their next steps. Brackenridge and other moderates argued openly for submitting to the federal government. A fire-breather promised "to defeat the first army that comes over the mountains and take their arms and baggage."[16] The meeting voted, thirty-two to twenty-three, for submission. The moderates had won, but the disaffected were still a sizable minority. The day after the commissioners' report of the vote reached Philadelphia, Washington ordered his troops to report for service. As soon as the commissioners returned to Philadelphia in the last week of September, the army moved westward.

Washington reviewed it in Carlisle, a town in central Pennsylvania just east of the Alleghenies. Here he was met by William Findley, a congressman from western Pennsylvania, another moderate, like Brackenridge, opposed to the tax, but dismayed by the course of events. Two civilians had already been killed near Carlisle by soldiers, and Findley urged Washington to keep the army from moving further. Washington assured him that disorder in the ranks would be curbed, but insisted that the government required "unequivocal *proofs* of absolute submission."[17] Washington visited two other staging areas in Virginia and then returned to Philadelphia. The army encountered no opposition on its march. It arrested one hundred and fifty people, all small-fry; twenty were indicted. Two men, both simpleminded, were convicted of treason and sentenced to death. Washington pardoned them.

One reason order was so easily restored was because of the implications of news that arrived in the midst of the crisis, from deep in the wilderness. During the last four years the administration had sent three expeditions across the Ohio River, to suppress Indians. The first two had ended in bloody debacles. The third, under General Anthony Wayne, won a major battle on the Miami River on August 20. The news reached

Washington at the end of September as he was on his way to Carlisle. Wayne's victory would give hard-pressed frontiersmen a chance to better themselves by moving west, and it showed that the federal government could do something *for* them as well as *to* them.

But the immediate cause of the collapse of the rebellion was the response of Washington. By not reacting hastily, he had let the most extreme ringleaders work themselves into an untenable position. Then, he had deployed overwhelming force—the Whiskey Rebellion army was five times as large as the army he had commanded at the Battle of Trenton—as well as the force of his presence. WASHINGTON IS EVER TRIUMPHANT, read a sign that greeted him in Carlisle. "THE MAN OF THE PEOPLE," wrote one soldier from Pennsylvania, "with a mien intrepid as that of Hector, yet graceful as that of Paris, moved slowly onward with his attending officers, nor once turned his eagle eye. . . ." When Washington gave a speech on the rebellion to Congress, one representative "felt a strange mixture of passions which I cannot describe. Tears started into my eyes, and it was with difficulty that I could suppress an involuntary effort to swear that I would support him."[18]

Washington felt it necessary to go to such lengths and to summon such emotions in part because he feared foreign meddling. British and Spanish colonial governors in Canada and Louisiana had been scheming for years to detach the frontier from the United States, with or without the permission of their home offices, and some frontiersmen had been engaged in schemes of their own. During the Whiskey crisis, men "of very decent manners and appearance" approached the British ambassador in Philadelphia to say that "they were dissatisfied with the government and were determined to separate from it." The ambassador turned them away and told Hamilton.[19]

Washington's main concern was not for Americans who

plotted with foreigners, but for America's understanding of it-self. He saw the Whiskey Rebellion as an attack on the legacy of the Revolution, all the more serious because it mimicked its arguments. Just as the Revolution had been provoked by taxes on tea and fees for stamps on legal documents, so the Rebellion was provoked by a whiskey excise. But the first laws had been passed for Americans, without consultation or consent. The last law had been passed by Americans, acting through their own government.

In a proclamation issued before he left Philadelphia for Carlisle, Washington summoned God, liberty, politics, and reason as witnesses to the justice of that government. ". . . the people of the United States have been permitted, under the Divine favor, in perfect freedom, after solemn deliberation, in an enlightened age, to elect their own Government. . . ." He defined the "contest" at hand as "whether a small proportion of the United States shall dictate to the whole Union. . . ." The key word was *dictate*. If Representative Findley and his constituents could persuade their fellow citizens that the excise was unwise or unjust, that would be a different matter. Until then, they could not casually flout the law or defy its administrators. ". . . if the laws are to be so trampled upon with impunity," Washington wrote in a letter, and "a minority . . . is to dictate to the majority, there is an end put at one stroke to republican government . . . for some other man or society may dislike another law and oppose it with equal propriety until all laws are prostrate, and everyone"—and here Washington produced one of the striking images which are even more striking because they are so rare in his writing—"will carve for himself."[20]

Self-government had two implications for Washington: the people ought to govern themselves, but then they really had to govern. They could not unmake their decisions arbitrarily. In the speech that drew the congressman's tears, Washington said that "the true principles of government and liberty" were "inseparabl[y]" united: "maintain[ing] the authority of the laws against licentious invasions" was as important as "defend[ing] . . . rights against usurpation."[21] As in Shays' Rebellion, Washington was even more concerned with the legitimacy of law than with order.

While excise men were being shot at in the Appalachians, John Jay, the Chief Justice of the Supreme Court, was in London meeting with the King and Queen and the Foreign Secretary, trying to untangle the knots in Anglo-American relations, some left over from the war's end eleven years earlier, some new. Jay's willingness to take months off to engage in diplomacy shows how little the Supreme Court had to do in 1794. But the treaty he signed in November gave Washington and American politicians a great deal to do in 1795 and 1796.

The struggle over Jay's Treaty occurred in two stages: Should the Senate and the President ratify it? Should the House vote the funds necessary to put it into effect? The second question raised an issue of self-government—of following through on one's own undertakings—akin to that raised by the Whiskey Rebellion. The more basic question, of what to make of the treaty in the first place, addressed another aspect of America's capacity to govern itself: Could a new, small nation maintain its independence in a world of contending empires? For Chief Justice Jay was not negotiating in a vacuum; the British were engaged in a world war, envenomed by ideology, with America's sometime ally, France. Could the United States avoid taking sides? Should it try?

The Republicans took the side of revolutionary France. Jefferson had written years earlier that the tree of liberty must be refreshed with the blood of tyrants, and French events after the fall of the Bastille struck him and his fellows as just such a refreshment. Republicans accordingly gave themselves over to a Francophile radical chic. When Louis XVI was guillotined in 1793, one wrote lightly in a Philadelphia paper that "*Capet* [Louis's family name] has lost his *Caput* [head]." A teacher at the University of Pennsylvania improved the climax of Henry V's speech before Harfleur, from "Cry—God for Harry! England! and St. George!" to "Cry—God for Freedom! France! and Robespierre!" Another revolutionary from afar, trying to produce a wedding announcement in the new French forms, was stumped by the problem of how to translate *citoyenne*, and finally came up with this: "On ———, *Citizen* ———was married to *Citess* ———." [22]

Hamilton and the Federalists felt free, now that the United States was independent of Britain, to admire it. Jefferson gloomily recorded an instance of this admiration in his journal in the spring of 1791. Vice-President Adams observed at a dinner party at Jefferson's lodgings that if the British constitution were reformed and purged of corruption, "it would be the most perfect constitution ever devised by the wit of man," to which Hamilton replied that if it were reformed and purged, it would become "*impracticable*"; it was "the most perfect government which ever existed" already. [23] Apart from after-dinner witticisms, the Hamiltonians saw Britain as a natural trading partner; they were disgusted by excesses in France and scarcely less disgusted by the rhetorical excesses of France's partisans in the United States.

Both France and Britain tried to manipulate the new country and their well-wishers within it. In the spring of 1793, a new French minister, Edmond Genet—Citizen Genet, to his friends—landed in Charleston. "It is beyond the power of figures or words to express the hugs and kisses that were lavished on him," wrote one Federalist journalist. ". . . very few parts, if any, of the Citizen's body, escaped a salute." [24] Genet claimed the right to arm private warships in American ports to prey on British shipping and grew so bumptious that by summer the Republicans had backed away from him. (When a new French government deposed Genet's faction and wanted to bring him home, undoubtedly to be executed, Washington offered him asylum.)

Hamilton, meanwhile, had been holding confidential conversations with the British minister for years, assuring him that "*we think in English* [emphasis Hamilton's]."[25] England, for its part, to the extent it thought of the United States at all, thought to keep its hand heavily involved in American affairs, particularly those concerning the frontier and trade. As of 1794, there were still one thousand British troops in eight forts on American soil. Anthony Wayne's victory in August had been won practically under the walls of a British outpost. On the high seas, Britain had forbidden American ships since the war from trading with its Caribbean colonies, though the prohibition was often flouted. Since the end of 1793, Britain had seized hundreds of American ships on the grounds that they were trading with France.

Washington tried to steer a course between these enthusiasms and dangers. In 1793, he declared America's neutrality with respect to the "belligerent powers." A year later, he picked the Anglophile Jay to negotiate a new treaty with Britain, at the same time selecting the Francophile Monroe as Minister to France. Monroe rewarded Washington's trust by communicating secretly in cipher with Jefferson, while Jay reported facts of particular delicacy not to the Secretary of State but to Hamilton. But Washington's balancing was not evenhandedness for its own sake, and it should not be judged by the misbehavior of his instruments. Washington's opinions of Britain and France reflected a view of the United States's place in the world that he had held as long as there had been a United States; indeed, he expressed it most notably in 1778, at the turning point of the Revolution.

After the battles of Saratoga and Monmouth Courthouse, with one British army vanquished in upstate New York and another bottled up in New York City, the Marquis de Lafayette had gone to Congress with a plan to strike while the iron was hot: the Americans should pick off British posts in western Canada, while the French sailed up the St. Lawrence and took Quebec. In a letter to Congress, Washington suggested that America try "something less extensive." In a private letter to Henry Laurens, President of Congress, he "unbosom[ed]" himself "on a point of the most delicate and important Nature," which had "alarm[ed] all my feelings for the true and permanent interests of my country." Would it be wise to introduce "a large body of French troops" into a part of Canada that was "attached to [France] by all the ties of blood, habits, manners, religion and former connexion of government"? Would it not pose "too great a temptation" to their new ally?

The context of Washington's doubts must be emphasized to give them their true force. Washington was in the midst of fighting an enemy whose wartime policies he abhorred. He considered Britain's use of Indians, Tory irregulars, and Hessian mercenaries barbarous. Jefferson had spoken for Washington and every revolutionary when he wrote, in the Declaration of Independence, that the British had been "deaf to the voice of justice and of consanguinity." At the same time, Washington had thanked "the Almighty ruler of the Universe" for the French alliance, and there was no Frenchman, indeed no man, whom he loved more than Lafayette. The childless general treated him as a son, while the young man, in ardent and fractured English, regarded Washington as "the salavation of his country and the admiration of the universe."

But these feelings had to give way to deeper considerations.

"Men are very apt to run into extremes," Washington wrote Laurens; "hatred to England may carry some into an excess of Confidence in France. . . . [B]ut it is a maxim founded on the universal experience of mankind, that no nation is to be trusted farther than it is bound by its interest; and no prudent statesman or politician will venture to depart from it. In our circumstances we ought to be particularly cautious; for we have not yet attained sufficient vigor and maturity to recover from the shock of any false step into which we may unwarily fall."[26] At moments of crisis, Washington appealed beyond interest to the feelings of his countrymen. But these feelings could not be relied upon to operate across national boundaries. In its dealings with the world, America must do what other nations did, and look to itself.

Washington may have been guided to this insight by the long perspective of his career. In the French and Indian War, he had fought Frenchmen at the side of Britons; in the Revolutionary War, he had done the reverse. The wheel had turned once; it might turn again. Washington may also have profited from lacking the cosmopolitan experiences of Jefferson, who had spent five years in Paris as a diplomat, or Hamilton, born and bred in the Caribbean. Washington's elder half-brothers had gone to school in England, but the only time George went overseas was when he accompanied one of them on a four-month trip to Barbados. The rest of his life had been spent in the colonies or the states and in the wilderness.

Whatever its source, his focus on the welfare of the United States helped him weather the storm that Jay had prepared for him.

The treaty Jay signed got the British out of their frontier forts; though it did not punish them for preying on American shipping, it provided that American merchants whose wares had been taken would be compensated, according to the judgment of arbitration tribunals; and it allowed American vessels to trade with the British West Indies, though it placed various restrictions on the size of the ships and the ultimate destination of their cargoes. No one in America learned of these details until March 1795, when a copy of the treaty finally arrived in Philadelphia. Washington decided not to make the text public until the Senate considered it, which it met to do in June.

Washington's policy of secrecy sprang from his own misgivings about the document. The pro-French party did not want any deal with Britain, short of a capitulation. Washington did not require so much, but he was not sure that Jay had gotten enough. In a private letter to Hamilton, who had returned to private life, he put his doubts in the mouths of unnamed "others [who] are of opinion that to have *no* commercial treaty would have been better, for this country, than the restricted one, agreed to. . . ."[27] If Britain wanted America's trade, why should America accept any limitations on it? The Senate, even with a pro-British majority, agreed with this argument and refused to accept the restrictions on Caribbean trade. It passed the rest of the treaty on a straight party line vote, twenty to ten, the bare two-thirds necessary. Washington, who was still weighing whether to sign it himself, decided to release the text on the first of July.

The treaty leaked out earlier, however, and in the worst possible way. A senator from Virginia sold his copy to the French ambassador, who gave it to Benjamin Franklin Bache, the philosopher's grandson and an incendiary newspaper editor. For months, all the public had known of the treaty were rumored hopes that it twisted the lion's tail or fears that it was a sellout. The unrealism of the hopes strengthened the fears. When Bache printed the text, the pro-French party gave way to wrath and shame. Jay was burned in effigy, and in Charleston a copy of his treaty was burned by the public hangman. Rioters in Philadelphia broke the British ambassador's windows, while rioters in New York nearly broke Hamilton's head, by stoning him as he spoke in the treaty's defense. ". . . the cry against the Treaty," wrote Washington to Hamilton, "is like that against a mad-dog."[28]

Washington went to Mount Vernon to collect his thoughts, but at the end of July the crisis was compounded by a brand-new one, as reflective of the political temper of the times as the turmoil in the streets. Timothy Pickering, who had replaced Knox as Secretary of War, wrote Washington urging him to return to Philadelphia "for a *special reason*, which can be communicated to you only in private." In the capital, Pickering presented himself at the President's mansion while Washington was meeting with Secretary of State Randolph. Washington left the room to ask Pickering what he had to communicate. Pickering pointed to the door of the room where Randolph sat, and said, "That man is a traitor."[29]

Pickering's accusation was founded on a secret dispatch of the previous French ambassador, which had been captured by a British man-of-war and passed along to the American government. The dispatch contained an unflattering analysis of the American political scene, supplied to the ambassador by the "precious confessions" of none other than the Secretary of State. Randolph was said to have accused the administration of provoking the Whiskey Rebellion in order to aggrandize power; he also seemed to have asked the ambassador for a French bribe to influence the outcome.

This puzzling tale came at a bad time for Randolph. William Pierce's sketches of delegates to the Constitutional Convention credited Randolph with "all the accomplishments of the Scholar, and the States-man . . . a most harmonious voice, a fine person, and striking manners."[30] One accomplishment he lacked was decision. He had presented the Virginia Plan to the

Convention and then refused to sign the Constitution, though he finally supported it back home. During the Whiskey Rebellion, his advice to Washington had been temporizing. In the present crisis, his counsel had been slow in coming and complicated when it came. On August 19, Washington presented Randolph with a copy of the dispatch at a Cabinet meeting, and asked him to explain it. Flustered by the sudden coldness of the man who had saved his reputation during the Revolution, Randolph resigned. Four months later, the former Secretary published a vindication which, while it acquitted his honor, gave no flattering or even intelligible account of his dealings with the French ambassador. When so many other figures in the administration had been carrying on private discussions with political allies and foreign diplomats, it may seem unfair that Washington singled Randolph out for scrutiny. But Randolph was Secretary of State; he had been caught, and caught at a moment of high tension.

The Randolph affair had been distressing to Washington personally and politically. Randolph had been the only Virginian in the Cabinet. His fall also marked another precedent for the administration—the first Secretary to resign under pressure. But it was a distraction from the business at hand. Washington had decided to sign the treaty before his confrontation with Randolph. One of his motives was the clamor in the streets: "I am excited to this resolution by the violent and extraordinary proceedings. . . ." Washington did not believe in government by uproar, in part because he feared what use foreign powers might make of it. ". . . it is in the interest of the French . . . to avail themselves of such a spirit, to keep *us* and *G. Britain* at variance; and they will, in my opinion, accordingly do it."[31] If Jay's handiwork was not the best of all possible treaties, it was not bad enough to risk such effects by rejecting it or fiddling with it.

The enemies of the treaty fell back on their political stronghold, the House of Representatives, where they made two arguments. One was that the House had a back-door power to block treaties, by refusing to vote the funds necessary to implement them. The antitreaty forces had hold of a real legal anomaly. The Constitution gave the power to make treaties to the President, with the advice and consent of the Senate. But it also gave the House the sole power to originate money bills. One delegate to the Convention had proposed to resolve the problem by giving the House a say on treaties. "As treaties . . . are to have the operation of laws, they ought to have the sanction of laws also."[32] The argument had been decisively rejected, on the grounds that the Senate, being smaller, was better able to keep the details of diplomacy secret.

The other tactic of the treaty's enemies was a frontal assault on the very notion of secrecy. In March 1796, the House asked Washington to turn over all instructions and correspondence related to Jay's negotiations, hoping to find politically embarrassing details. Washington answered five days later with a flat refusal, couched in a proud understatement. "Having been a member of the General Convention, and knowing the principles on which the Constitution was formed," he judged that to honor the House's request "would be to establish a dangerous precedent."[33]

As the House moved on to the question of appropriations, its antitreaty majority melted away. Hamilton had been busy in the newspapers, writing articles in the treaty's defense. The prospect of long-range peace with Britain had stimulated an economic boom, so that people who had disliked the treaty in theory came to approve of it in practice. The climax came at the end of April. Fisher Ames, a Federalist congressman from Massachusetts, left his sickbed to travel to Philadelphia to deliver an oration in the treaty's favor. "I entertain the hope, perhaps a rash one, that my strength will hold out to let me speak a few minutes," Ames told the House. He spoke for ninety. He painted a picture of the horrors of frontier war, if the House's second thoughts provoked the British to keep their forts. "In the day time, your path through the woods is ambushed; the darkness of midnight will glitter with the blaze of your dwellings. You are a father: the blood of your sons shall fatten your corn-field! You are a mother: the war-whoop shall wake the sleep of the cradle!" If the treaty went down, "even I, slender and almost broken as my hold on life is, may outlive the Government and Constitution of my country."[34]

The next day, the chairman of the Committee of the Whole, who had been opposed to the treaty, broke a tie vote to bring the appropriation before the House. It passed, by three votes. The chairman's brother-in-law stabbed him in the chest for his treachery. Ames kept his slender hold on life until 1808.

The Whiskey Rebellion arose in the woods, and the appropriations debate took place in the capital; one involved violence and intimidation, and the other employed learned arguments of constitutional theory. Yet the issue was the same. If a self-governing people decided legitimately to do a thing, could some people then prevent it from being done? Washington asserted, in both crises, that decisions could only be unmade in the same way they had been made.

The ratification of Jay's Treaty also assured that the country would not be tugged by sympathies with France into a showdown with Britain it could not afford. In 1798, running to extremes, the country waged an undeclared naval war with France. By 1812, veering back, it declared war on Britain. But by then, it was strong enough to absorb reverses as serious as the burning of Washington, D.C., thanks to Washington's prudence a decade and a half earlier.

Had Washington wanted a third term, there is no question that he would have been reelected once more. When Congress adjourned in the summer of 1796, Jefferson wrote glumly to Monroe that "one man outweighs them all in influence over the people. Republicanism must lie on its oars, resign the vessel to its pilot, and themselves to the course he thinks best for them."[35] But Washington had already set his own course toward retirement.

In May, Washington sent Hamilton a draft of a speech announcing his decision, recycling the text Madison had prepared four years earlier. He asked Hamilton to rewrite it or to submit a fresh draft in a "plain stile." Hamilton finished a new speech by July, which Washington preferred to his own, as being "more dignified . . . with less egotism." The President gave the text to a Philadelphia newspaper; the publisher later recalled that his editing of the punctuation was "very minute." The Farewell Address appeared in September, under a small headline, "To the PEOPLE of the United States/ Friends and fellow citizens," and signed "G. Washington."

The address restated many of the themes of Washington's administration and his career, most famously the doctrine of national self-interest and independence, first stated in his letter to Henry Laurens on the French in Canada: "The Nation, which indulges towards another an habitual hatred, or an habitual fondness, is in some degree a slave. It is a slave to its animosity or to its affection, either of which is sufficient to lead it astray from its duty and its interest."[36] But the most important fact about the Farewell Address was that it was made. Washington's last service to his country was to stop serving. He had often been compared to Cincinnatus, the half-legendary hero of the Roman Republic, who returned to his farm after saving his country in wartime. The popularity of the comparison arose from a vogue among Americans of the eighteenth century for playing at noble Romans. But, as Americans well knew, there had also been ignoble Romans, many of whom had played at being noble. The Republic that Cincinnatus once saved was finally subverted by emperors who carefully maintained republican forms, while employing a Cincinnatian rhetoric of modesty and diffidence. "You all did see that on the Lupercal/ I thrice presented him a kingly crown/ Which he did thrice refuse," Shakespeare's Marc Anthony said of Caesar. "Was this ambition?" It was, though it was left to Augustus to fufill it. Washington had professed diffidence and proclaimed his own unworthiness since 1775, with such evident sincerity that his countrymen had showered powers on his head. The fulfillment of all the years of saying how reluctant he was to step forward was to step down.

When he left office five months after the Farewell Address was published, the merchants of Philadelphia gave him a banquet in a hall adorned by an "emblematical" painting.

"The principal was a female figure large as life, representing America, seated on an elevation composed of sixteen* marble steps. At her left side, stood the federal shield and eagle, and at her feet, lay the cornucopiae; in her right hand, she held the Indian [pipe] of peace supporting the cap of liberty: in the perspective appeared the temple of fame; and on her left hand, an altar dedicated to public gratitude, upon which incense was burning. In her left hand she held a scroll inscribed valedictory; and at the foot of the altar lay a plumed helmet and sword, from which a figure of General Washington, large as life, appeared, retiring down the steps, pointing with his right hand to the emblems of power which he had resigned, and with his left to a beautiful landscape representing Mount Vernon, in front of which oxen were seen harnessed to the plough. Over the general appeared a *Genuis*, placing a wreath of laurels on his head."[37]

---

* Vermont, Kentucky, and Tennessee had joined the original states.

The artwork may have been laughable, but the artist had grasped the essential point: Washington was worthy of honor because the last thing he had done with power was to resign it. Others grasped it, even abroad. George III said his retirement from the presidency, coupled with his resignation as Commander in Chief fourteen years earlier, "placed him in a light the most distinguished of any man living," and that he was "the greatest character of the age." The greatest character of the next age agreed. Though their careers overlapped, Washington was not aware of Napoleon, who was a French officer during the 1790s. But Napoleon was aware of him. After he had seized a crown and a continent and lost them both, Napoleon said, "They wanted me to be another Washington."[38]

John Adams was inaugurated as second President on March 4, 1797. Washington had preceded him to the hall and sat on the dais with Jefferson, the Vice-President-elect, as Adams spoke. When the new President finished and left, Washington motioned to Jefferson to go next. The two Virginians had known each other since 1769, when Washington had been thirty-seven years old and Jefferson only twenty-six. From long habit and lingering respect, Jefferson now held back. But Washington gestured again, in a manner not to be ignored. The younger man was now Vice-President and must go first.

It was not quite the end of Washington's public career. In the summer of 1798, President Adams tapped his predecessor to command the army, in case of a French invasion. (Embittered by America's negotiations with Britain, France had been raiding American shipping and dealing high-handedly with American diplomats.) Washington accepted the assignment willingly—he designed a new uniform for himself and passed brisk judgments on proposed officers: "What could have induced the nomination of Walt[on] White . . . ? Of all the character in the Revolutionary Army, I believe one more obnoxious to the Officers who composed it could not have been hit upon. . . ." He took the assignment all the more willingly because he had come to believe that the French were incorrigible enemies, and because, at the age of 66, the political moderation to which he had adhered throughout his presidency had begun to desert him: the Republicans, he wrote Patrick Henry, "prefer . . . the interest of France to the Welfare of their own Country." Even so, when Washington got a letter that winter from Joel Barlow, an American poet living in Paris, suggesting that a new French government might be willing to settle differences peaceably, he forwarded it to Adams, in the hope "that it would become a mean, however small, of restoring Peace and Tranquillity to the United States upon honorable and dignified terms: which I am persuaded is the ardent desire of all the friends of this rising Empire."

It was a moving letter in the twilight of his life, an affirmation of his policies against what had become his inclinations. He wrote a more moving one some months later, after Adams had announced that he was opening his own negotiations with France. The Federalists were divided and dismayed by the news, and their hard-liners—including most of Adams's cabinet—shared their doubts freely with Washington. He admitted to James McHenry, the Secretary of War, that he had "for some time past viewed the political concerns of the United States with an anxious and painful eye." But, he concluded, "the vessel is afloat or very nearly so, and considering myself as a passenger only, I shall trust to the mariners whose duty it is to watch, to steer it into a safe port."[39] He could not have known it, but he had used the very metaphor Jefferson had used in his letter to Monroe three years earlier—with the difference that he now took himself out of the pilot's chair. Putting power aside means putting yourself aside too. At the end of his life, he let his handiwork take control of him.

Character

NATURE

The list of personal traits that enabled Washington to do what he did is long and various and ranges from a youthful bout with smallpox, which immunized him against the disease, to a youthful fondness for Seneca, which may have immunized him against temper tantrums. But the important qualities that shaped his reactions to experience, and people's reactions to him, fall into a few categories. Washington's character may be compared to a three-storied building. The ground floor consisted of what was given to him by nature and cultivated by the conditions of his life: his physicality and his temperament. His form was imposing, and his temper was dangerous. Displaying the one, and controlling the other, were essential to his success as a leader.

In 1760, Captain George Mercer, who had been Washington's aide in the Virginia militia, wrote a long description of him. "[He is] straight as an Indian, measuring six feet two inches in his stockings* and weighing 175 pounds. . . . His

---

* At his death he was measured at six feet three and one-half inches.

frame is padded with well-developed muscles, indicating great strength. His bones and joints are large, as are his hands and feet. He is wide shouldered but has not a deep or round chest; is neat waisted, but is broad across the hips and has rather long legs and arms. His head is well-shaped, though not large, but is gracefully poised on a superb neck. A large and straight rather than a prominent nose; blue gray penetrating eyes which are widely separated and overhung by a heavy brow. His face is long rather than broad, with high round cheek bones, and terminates in a good firm chin. He has clear though rather colorless pale skin which burns with the sun. A pleasing and benevolent though a commanding countenance, dark brown hair which he wears in a cue. His mouth is large and generally firmly closed, but which from time to time discloses some defective teeth. His features are regular and placid with all the muscles of his face under perfect control, though flexible and expressive of deep feeling when moved by emotions. In conversation he looks you full in the face, is deliberate, deferential, and engaging. His demeanor at all times composed and dignified. His movements and gestures are graceful, his walk majestic, and he is a splendid horseman."[1]

Some of the physical details of this portrait changed over the course of Washington's life: his defective teeth came out, to be replaced by various sets of almost equally defective false teeth, and he gained weight, though only up to a point: by the time he was fifty-one, he weighed two hundred and nine pounds; fifteen years later, he weighed one pound more. Mercer does not mention the light pockmarks on his nose, souvenirs of his disease, probably because so many people in the eighteenth century bore them. But the general impression of Washington's appearance that Mercer gives is one that would be registered by observers for the next forty years, often in the identical words: "Washington," wrote an English visitor in 1796, "has something uncommonly majestic and commanding in his walk, his address, his figure, and his countenance."[2] It was not an impression of glamour, or of beauty—some of his features (the large hands, the shallow chest) were potentially unattractive—but of the presence of the whole figure. Many of us have bodies which sit or stand dully or droop like suits on wire hangers. Washington's body organized the space around it, as a dancer's arms or legs seem to stretch beyond the tips of the fingers or toes. When he entered a room or a crowd, he was noticed.

Soldiers were very aware of his comings and his doings. Dr. James Thacher, the medical officer of the American army, noted that when he first took command in 1775, the men were "much gratified" to be able to pick him out from among his aides at a glance. Lafayette's rapturous description of him at the Battle of Monmouth Courthouse, even after making allowance for hero worship, explains why his men considered him heroic. "His graceful bearing on horseback, his calm and deportment which still retained a trace of displeasure . . . were all calculated to inspire the highest degree of enthusiasm. . . . I thought then as now that I had never beheld so superb a man."[3]

Women also took note of him. In her letter urging him to serve a second term, Mrs. Eliza Powel, citing his looks among his qualifications for office, argued that his physical stature enhanced his political stature. ". . . your very figure is calculated to inspire confidence with people whose simple good sense appreciates the noblest qualities of mind with the heroic form." "You had prepared me to entertain a favorable opinion of him," wrote Abigail Adams to her husband after she first met Washington, "but I thought the one half was not told me. . . . Those lines of Dryden instantly occurd to me

'Mark his Majestick fabrick! he's a temple
Sacred by birth, and built by hands divine
His Souls the deity that lodges there.
Nor is the pile unworthy of the God.' "

Years later, John Adams compared Washington, with less enthusiasm, to "the Hebrew sovereign chosen because he was taller by the head than the other Jews." Washington was certainly a head taller than Adams.[4]

Mercer began his description by calling him "straight as an Indian." This comparison also recurred over the years. "Had he been born in the forests," wrote Gilbert Stuart, who painted him in his sixties, "he would have been the fiercest man among the savage tribes."[5] This was a way for Europeans and even Americans (who knew Indians better) to add a dash of local color to figures they associated with the frontier. But the frontier was real, and Washington had spent more time in it than many of his contemporaries—more, certainly, than any subsequent president, except perhaps Andrew Jackson. He had fought with and against Indians, and he entertained them in the presidential mansion. The simile may have been romantic, but it was not fanciful.

Washington's body commanded attention because of its prowess as well as its appearance. A visitor to Mount Vernon in 1772 remembered tossing an iron bar on the lawn with some young men, when Washington asked "to be shown the pegs that marked the bounds of our effort; then smiling, and without putting off his coat, held out his hand for the missile." Washington's toss "str[uck] the ground far, very far beyond our utmost limits . . . the Colonel, on retiring, pleasantly observed, 'When you beat my pitch, young gentlemen, I'll try again.'" Garry Wills noted that the anecdote is already taking the shape of a legend, but there is no need to doubt it. Washington boasted that he had once thrown a stone up to the Natural Bridge, a 215-foot-high rock arch in the Shenandoah Valley.[6] His workaday feats of strength and stamina were scarcely less remarkable. During the War, he could stay awake and on horseback for days at a stretch. On his first expedition to the Pennsylvania wilderness, he walked for a week through snowy, pathless woods, fell off a raft into an ice-choked river, spent the night on an island, and then pressed on to a trading post. His traveling companion, a frontiersman, came down with frost-bite; he did not.

Many of his pastimes were active and such as would show him off. He learned to dance when he was fifteen, paying three shillings ninepence to attend a dancing school, and he practiced what he had learned until his late fifties. During his first term as president, he carefully described the balls thrown in his honor and the number and comeliness of the women in attendance. "There were about seventy-five well dressed and many of them very handsome ladies" at Portsmouth, New Hampshire, "among whom . . . were a greater proportion with much blacker hair than are usually seen in the southern states."[7]

Another activity that was part hobby, part simple necessity was riding. Jefferson (who, as a Virginian, knew what he was talking about) called him "the best horseman of his age, and the most graceful figure that could be seen on horseback." Washington's hours in the saddle are evident even in nonequestrian pictures of him: Trumbull's portrait after the battle of Trenton clearly shows a pair of well-developed thighs. When I showed it to a body builder, she said: "*Nice* quads." A typical day at Mount Vernon began with a circuit of his farms. During his first year as president, he would ride from southern Manhattan to Morningside Heights and back, a round-trip of fourteen miles. "He rode, as he did every thing, with ease, elegance, and with power," remembered George Custis, his stepgrandson. His "perfect and sinewy frame . . . gave him such a surpassing grip with his knees, that a horse might as soon disencumber itself of the saddle, as of such a rider." Washington tested his firmness in the saddle in many a fox hunt. He acquired a pack in 1767; two years later, a month in his diary during hunting season reads like this: "Jan. 4, Fox hunting; 10,

Fox hunting; 11, Fox hunting; 12, Went out in the morning with the hounds; 16, Went a ducking; 17, Fox hunting; 18, Fox hunting; 19, Fox hunting; 20, Fox hunting; 21, Fox hunting; 25, Hunting below Accatinck; 28, Went a Hunting. . . ." The hunts could last seven hours. Washington followed his pack closely and was "always in at the death . . . yielding to no man the honor of the brush."[8]

In egalitarian ages, riding carries sinister political connotations. A "man on horseback" is a would-be dictator. An English Puritan of the seventeenth century declared that Providence did not "send a few men into the world, ready booted and spurred to ride, and millions ready saddled and bridled to be ridden"—a sentiment echoed in the nineteenth century in Jefferson's last public pronouncement.[9] What the egalitarians ignored is the appeal of the centaur. A spectator identifies with both the rider and the mount, admiring the rider's control of a beautiful and powerful animal and appreciating the guidance of knowing legs and hands. Certainly the soldier retreating across the Assunpink under enemy fire appreciated Washington's firmness in the saddle. Today such feelings can only be savored indirectly, from westerns; in Washington's day, it was still possible to experience the emotion without denial.

Washington displayed his figure in uniforms. He had a lifelong interest in shows and spectacles of all kinds—plays, circuses, puppet shows, exhibitions of wild animals—but the show with the longest run was himself. In August 1755, after Braddock's army had been destroyed in the wilderness, Virginia raised a regiment to defend itself and put Washington in command. Children's books still say that Washington had advised Braddock to take his men out of red coats and dress them in forest colors—advice the Englishman supposedly ignored. How likely this is may be judged from the uniform Washington designed to wear at the head of his own regiment, which wasn't that of a guerilla: "the coat to be faced and cuffed with scarlet and trimmed with silver; a scarlet waistcoat with silver lace; blue breeches; and a silver laced hat." He designed his last uniform during the war scare of 1798: "a blue coat with yellow buttons and gold epaulettes (each having three silver stars). . . . The coat to be without lapels, and embroidered on the cape, cuffs, and pockets. A white plume in the hat to be a further distinction."[10] Washington's waistcoats and plumes were not "natural," but they were not the affectations of a dandy. He wore uniforms because he was a soldier or—as when he appeared before the Continental Congress in military garb—because he hoped to become one. He looked good in them because he looked good. Men responded to the spectacle.

"It is an interesting question," wrote Thoreau, "how far men would retain their relative rank if they were divested of their clothes. Could you, in such a case, tell surely of any company of civilized men which belonged to the most respected class?" George Orwell, going even further, argued that leaders are, if anything, remarkable for their "quite fantastic ugliness." A gallery of "the great ones of the earth," circa 1944, he wrote, would include "Mussolini with his scrubby dewlap, the chinless de Gaulle, the stumpy short-armed Churchill, Gandhi with his long sly nose and huge bats' ears. . . ."[11] Washington would stand out from both Thoreau's locker-room line-up and Orwell's rogues' gallery, because he passed the first test of politics.

The body is the basic unit of all human intercourse, including politics. Civilization modifies or suppresses the fact, in the interest of cultivating other qualities. Yet even rulers who are intelligent, prudent, or visionary must make a sensual impact if they are to lead. If their bodies cannot command attention, they must compel it by secondary physical means, such as eloquence, or by props—masks, regalia, Air Force One. (Gandhi used the most ostentatious props of any modern leader—the dhoti and the walking stick.) Republics, which profess to dispense with the props, fall back on the primal importance of the body. Sixteen of America's presidents have fought in battle, the ultimate physical test (Washington, Monroe, Jackson, William Henry Harrison, Taylor, Pierce, Grant, Hayes, Garfield, Benjamin Harrison, McKinley, Theodore Roosevelt, Truman, Eisenhower, Kennedy, Bush); two who did not were college athletes (Ford, Reagan). Americans admired Franklin Roosevelt for his struggles with polio, but they would not have admired him, as a leader, so much if he had not also been handsome and dashing (and if he had not carefully concealed how crippled he actually was). Washington had physical authority in its simplest form, and though he improved it with exercise and adornment, they functioned as supplements, not substitutes. He "has so much martial dignity in his deportment that you would distinguish him to be a general and a soldier from among ten thousand people," wrote Benjamin Rush, a physician and politician, in October 1775. "There is not a king in Europe that would not look like a valet de chambre by his side."[12]

Washington's temperament is more complicated than his "majestic fabrick," though the two had some relation. Just as big dogs are less excitable than small ones, so Washington showed something of a big man's ease and composure—up to a point. He enjoyed company and entertaining, especially at Mount Vernon; accounts of his discomfort at the dinner table come from his presidency, when the table was not truly his own. Gentlemen were expected to entertain, by virtue of their station in life, but had he not taken to his role, guests would not so often have described him as "affable" or "amiable." He had one of the sure signs of a capacious spirit, the ability to laugh at another's jokes (he favored surprising scenes and ironic juxtapositions). He enjoyed Gouverneur Morris's wit, even though he lectured him; until other aspects of their characters assumed prominence, he enjoyed the wit of Charles Lee and Benedict Arnold. A subtler mark of his hospitality of mind appears in his letters, in the changes his style underwent depending on whom he was addressing. When corresponding with Lafayette, his own prose took on some of Lafayette's ingenuous warmth. One of his most charming letters was written to a man who most needed to be charmed: an amateur composer. ". . . what, alas! can I do to support [your music]?" he wrote Francis Hopkinson, who had sent him a set of pieces for the harpsichord. "I can neither sing one of the songs, nor raise a single note on any instrument to convince the unbelieving, but I have, however, one argument which will prevail with persons of true taste (at least in America), I can tell them that it is the production of Mr. Hopkinson." "[He] has so happy a faculty of appearing to accomodate and yet carrying his point," wrote Abigail Adams, "that if he was really not one of the best-intentioned men in the world, he might be a very dangerous one."[13]

His temperament had its raw edges, however, and when they were incautiously touched, he could become dangerous to those around him. George Mercer had noted that Washington's skin was pale and easily burned; it was also thin. One English guest at Mount Vernon, after taking due note of his "affability and accomodation," added that there was "a certain anxiety on his countenance which marks extreme sensibility." Washington was extremely sensitive to hostile criticism. Though he came in for less of it than any other President, he did get some, chiefly from a handful of Republican editors, who called him variously a gambler, a cheapskate, a horsebeater, a dictator, and "a most horrid swearer and blasphemer." "I think he feels those things more than any person I ever yet met with,"[14] wrote Jefferson after Washington had been complaining to him of the tone of Philip Freneau's *National Gazette*. Jefferson knew well what Washington was complaining of, since he employed Freneau in the State Department.

Like many sensitive people, he had a temper. He was passionate for distinction and for having his way, and when he was frustrated his affability could vanish. Gilbert Stuart likened him not just to an Indian, but to a fierce Indian. Another English guest at Mount Vernon, this one a comic actor, noted in his face a "compression of the mouth and [an] indentation of the brow . . . suggesting habitual conflict with and mastery over passion. . . ."[15] It is interesting that a portrait painter and an actor, two professional students of character and appearance, saw the same thing in him. Washington's passions had shown themselves for all to see when his soldiers retreated at Kip's Bay and when Charles Lee retreated at Monmouth Courthouse: certainly Lee felt he had seen them.

But Washington's temper and willfulness were not detected only by experts nor displayed only in battlefield crises. They were a lifelong presence, in war and in peace. When he was sixteen years old and had gotten his first job surveying the holdings of his in-laws and neighbors, the Fairfaxes, Thomas, Lord Fairfax, the head of the family, sent an assessment of his young employee to Washington's mother. "I wish I could say that he governs his temper." Washington's first tangle with the French eight years later showed him to be headstrong and high-handed, as well as bold and enterprising. The judgment of Britain's agent for Indian affairs (that he was "too ambitious of acquiring all the honor") has been quoted above. One of Britain's Indian allies who had been with him "complained very much" of Washington's behavior; he "command[ed] Indians as his slaves" and "would by no means take advice . . . but was always driving them on to fight by his directions."[16]

These were the excesses of a youth. But Hamilton wrote of the forty-eight-year-old Washington, after four years of service on his staff, that he was "remarkable [neither] for delicacy nor for good temper." Hamilton was in a bad temper when he wrote that, for Washington had just chewed him out. "Two days ago, the General and I passed each other on the stairs" at headquarters. "He told me he wanted to speak to me. I answered that I would wait upon him immediately." Two minutes later, by Hamilton's own count, "I met him at the head of the stairs where, accosting me in an angry tone, 'Colonel Hamilton,' said he, 'you have kept me waiting at the head of the stairs these ten minutes. I must tell you, sir, you treat me with disrespect.' "[17] Hamilton resigned then and there, as he said, "without petulancy," which was obviously untrue, though, to do him justice, he was not the only petulant man on the staircase.

In 1793, at the height of Citizen Genet's trajectory, a pro-French satire describing Washington's execution by guillotine was mentioned at a Cabinet meeting. Jefferson recorded what happened next with a seismologist's care. Washington became "much inflamed; got into one of those passions when he cannot command himself; . . . [said] that he had never repented but once having slipped the moment of resigning his office, and that was every moment since; that *by God* he had rather be in his grave than in his present situation; that he had rather be on his farm than to be made *Emperor of the World.* . . . That that *rascal Freneau* sent him three of his papers every day, as if he thought he would become the distributor of his papers, and that he could see in this nothing but an impudent design to insult him. He ended in this high tone."[18]

Late in 1795, when Edmund Randolph's vindication of himself appeared in print, Timothy Pickering witnessed a similar scene. Washington enumerated Randolph's defects, cried "he has written and published this," and threw the pamphlet to the floor. There are problems with the details of Pickering's account, as there are with Hamilton's. Pickering was remembering an incident many years after the fact; Hamilton wrote two days later, but in a fit of pique. But both stories agree with Jefferson's and with Jefferson's considered judgment, in his last, formal portrait of the man, that Washington's "temper was naturally irritable and high-toned"; when "it broke its bonds, he was most tremendous in his wrath."[19]

The testimony of Washington's three political associates has something else in common: each of the outbursts they recount came to a quick and definite end. As Hamilton himself admitted, "less than an hour" after their clash, Washington sent an aide to tell Hamilton how highly he thought of him, and to express the hope that a talk between them might heal the breach. Although Hamilton rejected the olive branch, Washington gave him an infantry brigade to command, and entrusted him with a crucial attack at Yorktown eight months later. The topic under discussion when Washington's guillotining came up had been whether to embarrass France by publicizing certain of Genet's indiscretions. Although the satire that set Washington off was the work of French sympathizers, he decided when he became calm again to continue current policy, which was to be discreet. He would not respond to provocation by needlessly provoking a foreign power. After spurning Randolph's vindication, Washington "calmly resumed his seat. The storm was over."

So it was when the Senate dawdled over the Creek treaty. After slipping into a fret, Washington returned another day, "serene and placid."[20]

Anger sometimes burns itself out. Emotional storms can clear the air. But anger can also feed itself, like a crack in a dam, when the first leak brings on a deluge. The pattern of closure in Washington's outbursts suggests a pattern of deliberate control. They ended because he willed them to end. Considering the problems that arose during eight and a half years as Commander in Chief and eight years as President, there must have been many storms which were controlled before they burst out. Virtually every observer who noted Washington's temper also noted the close rein he kept on it—including Washington himself. Henry Lee, a family friend, once told the Washingtons that the painter Stuart said his subject had a temper. Martha Washington exclaimed that Stuart had been out of line to say so. Lee finished the story: Stuart had added that the temper was under "wonderful control." "Mr. Stuart is right," Washington remarked.[21] Right on both counts.

Washington's temperament was like the horses he rode. A high tone can be anger, it can also be courage. The young man who brushed aside Indian advice and rushed to defeat was the same man who, later in the war, stepped between the muskets of his men as they shot at each other and, in the next war, led his men up to the enemy's line on the road to Princeton and gave the command to fire. A sense of latent anger, of suppressed force, can be an aspect of courage, an emphasis and a highlight. The "trace of displeasure" in Washington's deportment at Monmouth Courthouse, lingering from his encounter with Charles Lee, made him all the more impressive to Lafayette. But if spirit is to manifest itself as courage, and not flow away in pointless eruptions, it must be channeled and directed.

The few odd features of Washington's body were integrated into a powerful whole by grace and demeanor, by the way he moved and carried himself. Physical traits balanced each other like counterweights. Passions are not so responsive to mutual influence; left to themselves, they jostle together, each seeking only its own fulfillment. In order to integrate them successfully, Washington had to draw on other areas of his character.

MORALS

A man's stature and his temperament are more or less given to him by nature, but good behavior is something that must be pointed out. If he follows a good example regularly enough, then good actions may become "second" nature to him. The intersection of virtue, habit, and precept is pinpointed in the word "morals," which simultaneously opens out to morality, right and wrong, and delves down into manners, customs, mores. It is the second story of Washington's character. Throughout his career as a leader, he wrestled with the problem of national self-government. Morals were the way he governed himself.

Washington's contemporaries were greatly interested in encouraging goodness by good advice, in adults as well as in children. Franklin related in his *Autobiography* how as a young man he drew up a list of thirteen virtues which he wished to acquire and a program for practicing them. "I was surprised to find myself so much fuller of faults than I had imagined; but I had the satisfaction of seeing them diminish." One of the most popular sources of guidance in his day, and one that Washington might have cited as an influence on him, were the virtues of the Romans. Historians and biographers have certainly cited them. "So everyone" in the American government, write Stanley Elkins and Eric McKitrick, "was more or less Roman. George Washington ranked first, and John Adams was the next Roman below him."[1]

For all their artistic and philosophical brilliance, the Greeks were failures at politics; Hamilton, in the *Federalist*, expressed "horror and disgust" at the "distractions with which they were agitated." The Romans captured the American imagination because they had done what the Americans themselves hoped to do—sustain an extensive republic over a course of centuries. So the society of Revolutionary War officers called themselves the Cincinnati; "president," "congress," and "senate" were all Roman terms. But the Roman example was also cautionary, for when they lost their virtue, they slid into empire. When Franklin said, in response to a question from Eliza Powel, that the constitutional convention had produced "a republic, if you can keep it," he and she would have remembered that the Romans had failed to keep theirs.[2]

Washington encountered the Roman atmosphere long before the revolution. He bandied Roman allusions with the Fairfaxes: William Fairfax, who managed the family's holdings, wrote letters to Colonel Washington at his frontier post decorated with occasional philosophical reflections, including the reminder that his trials as an officer were, after all, less onerous than Caesar's. But Washington's extended exposure to Roman virtue, beyond sententious tags, came from two popular works by or about Romans, filtered through a contemporary English sensibility: *Seneca's Morals*, a collection of moral essays by the first-century philosopher and playwright, translated in 1682 by

Roger L'Estrange, an English pamphleteer, and Joseph Addison's 1713 drama, *Cato*. Washington acquired a copy of *Seneca's Morals* in his late teens, and he quoted lines and phrases from *Cato* all his life.

The book and the play teach the consoling lesson—consoling to writers, anyway—that mediocre work can attract the attention of great men. *Seneca's Morals* is the more interesting. It stayed in print in the English-speaking world until well into the nineteenth century, partly because of L'Estrange's lively style, partly because Seneca's earnest moralizing has always made him popular with Christians. One of his thoughts on fortitude shines like a light: "He that has lost one battle, hazards another." There is no way of knowing whether the future general read that particular sentence, though he could hardly have missed what Seneca/L'Estrange had to say about anger, since an entire essay was devoted to the subject and titled simply, "On Anger": "the most outrageous, brutal, dangerous, and intractable of all passions, the most loathsome and unmannerly, nay, the most ridiculous too. . . . If I were to describe it, I would . . . dress it up as the poets represent the furies, with whips, snakes and flames: it should be sour, livid, full of scars, and wallowing in gore, raging up and down, destroying, grinning, bellowing and pursuing, sick of all other things, and most of all of itself." Perhaps Washington took these vivid denunciations of his own particular passion as a warning; one of William Fairfax's letters, written several years after Washington got the book, compliments him on his "practice" of a "philosophic" state of mind.[3]

Addison's drama about the last stand of Cato the Younger, a republican politician of the first century B.C. who committed suicide rather than submit to Caesar, is smooth as a board and just as stiff, unreadable today except by intellectual archeologists, but it was wildly popular in eighteenth-century England

and America, thanks to the maxims that the barely distinguishable characters let fall. (As Dr. Johnson wrote, we do not care what the characters "are doing or what they are suffering; we wish only to know what they have to say.")[4] Patrick Henry's "Give me liberty or give me death" echoed one of their sentiments; so did the last words of Nathan Hale. Two others lines of the play—"Thy steady temper . . . can look on guilt, rebellion, fraud, and Caesar, in the calm light of mild philosophy" and "When vice prevails . . . the post of honor is a private station"—were favorites of Washington's. As a young man, he alluded to *Cato* in a letter to William Fairfax's daughter-in-law, Sally, coyly comparing himself and her to the play's frustrated lovers. As a man, he had *Cato* performed at Valley Forge.

Cato makes a passing case against impassioned eloquence, which fit with Washington's practice as a speaker. One of the villains announces early on that he will

> conceal
> My thoughts in passion ('tis the the surest way);
> I'll bellow out for Rome, and for my country,
> And mouth at Caesar, till I shake the senate.

He does not fool Cato, however.

> Let not a torrent of impetuous zeal
> Transport thee thus beyond the bounds of reason;
> True fortitude is seen in great exploits,
> That justice warrants, and that wisdom guides;
> All else is towering frenzy and distraction.

Such wooden moralizing—as if *Hamlet* were about Polonius—suggests why *Cato* is unlikely to be revived, though to be fair to Addison and his American admirers, there is one pair of lines in the play that is arresting and truly noble:

> 'Tis not in mortals to command success,
> But we'll do more, Sempronius, we'll deserve it.[5]

Considering how highly Washington esteemed the noble Romans, at least in their Anglo-Roman incarnations—he never learned Latin or any other foreign language—it would be presumptuous to be ironic about their literary shortcomings if there were not other ironies implicit in their example. Politically speaking, Cato and Seneca failed as badly as the Greeks. For all Cato's virtue, Caesar wins, while the historical Seneca worked for the emperor Nero, of all people, suggesting that if philosophers spend too much time practicing their state of mind, they may lose sight of what is going on around them.

More important, aside from a few detachable arguments and a general air of moral striving, the noble Romans do not much resemble Washington. He took them as an inspiration and perhaps also as a corrective to certain of his own flaws. But inspirations can be quite vague, and a corrective or compensating excess is not necessarily what one becomes after administering it. The "philosophic" state of mind, as described by Seneca, can seem inert and torpid. "The true felicity of life is to be free from perturbations. . . . Not to amuse ourselves with either hopes or fears, but to rest satisfied with what we have, which is abundantly sufficient; for he that is so, wants nothing."[6] Washington loved Mount Vernon as much as anything else in his life, but if that was all he had loved or cared for, he could have easily rested there.

Addison's Cato, on the other hand, sacrifices all for his country, but in a spirit that glories in its severity. In Act III, Cato quells a mutiny by reminding the rebellious soldiers of *his* sufferings.

Have you forgotten Libya's burning waste? . . .
Who was the first to explore the untrodden path,
When life was hazarded in every step?
Or, fainting in the long laborious march,
When, on the banks of an unlooked-for stream,

You sunk the river with repeated draughts,
Who was the last in all your host that thirsted? . . .
Hence, worthless men! hence! and complain to Caesar,
You could not undergo the toil of war,
Nor bear the hardships that your leader bore.

The mutineers are as abashed as the officers at Newburgh would be in 1783, after Washington quelled their unrest. But what a different appeal Washington would make to them. Unlike Cato, he would stress what he and they had undergone together. ". . . as I was *among* the first who embarked in the cause . . . As I have never left *your* side . . . As I have been the constant *companion* and witness of your distresses . . ." Perhaps for this reason, the meeting at Newburgh ended in reconciliation, while Addison's hero orders his restive soldiers executed.

When by just vengeance guilty mortals perish,
The gods behold their punishment with pleasure.

The trouble with the Roman virtues, or those that Washington studied, is that they are inhumane. As *Cato* approaches its climax, one of the republican remnant argues for surrender, saying that, after all, Caesar has "the virtues of humanity." "Curse on his virtues!" Cato replies, "they've undone his country."[7] The noble Romans offer to solve life's problems by keeping others at arm's length, or by hectoring them—or by worse. Eighteenth-century France took its Romans not from Addison's inert play, but from Jacques-Louis David's showstopper paintings: Junius Brutus receiving the bodies of his own sons, whom he has ordered executed for political plotting; the Horatii swearing to fight the enemies of Rome to the death, even though they are in-laws. The French had more serious Romans and took them more seriously. As they showed them, so they reaped.

One sign that Washington unconsciously suspected that he was not any kind of Roman appears in a postwar letter to Jefferson, about a plan for a statue in his honor. Would the marble Washington wear a toga? Though unwilling to oppose his judgment "to the taste of connoisseurs," Washington suggested "some little deviation in favor of the modern costume," immediately citing a connoisseur to back him up. "This taste, which has been introduced in painting by Mr. West [Benjamin West, an American-born artist who lived in London], I understand is received with applause, and prevails extensively."[8] He did not want to copy Roman dress, and for all his reverence, he did not completely copy their behavior.

Jefferson had the last word on Washington's relationship with the noble Romans in 1795, when the House was going head to head with the President over Jay's treaty, and he took it from *Cato*. "Curse on his virtues," Jefferson wrote to Madison, "they've undone his country."[9] He wasn't right about the treaty or the country, but he was right about Washington's virtues and their limited resemblance to the Anglo-Roman ideal.

A set of precepts that meant much more to Washington and that has drawn the attention of historians, though perhaps not enough, was one that he had copied out by hand by the age of sixteen, "The Rules of Civility and Decent Behavior in Company and in Conversation."[10] They outline a different map of morality and a different constellation of virtues. During his second term, Mrs. Henrietta Liston, the wife of the British ambassador, noted that Washington had "perfect good breeding, & a correct knowledge of even the etiquette of a court," though how he had acquired it, "heaven knows." Jefferson, Adams, and Franklin had lived in Europe for years; no wonder they knew their way around a drawing room. Mrs. Liston did not know that Washington had been practicing his manners for half a century, as well as the morals that they implied.

The "Rules of Civility"—one hundred and ten in all—are based on a set composed by French Jesuits in 1595. In 1640, an

English translation appeared, ascribed to Francis Hawkins, the twelve-year-old son of a doctor. (The precocious Hawkins was supposed to have made his translation four years earlier.) The Hawkins version of the rules went through eleven editions over the next three decades. How they got to Virginia in the middle of the next century is unknown. Presumably a schoolmaster or tutor made Washington write them out, in part as an exercise in penmanship. Washington's copy is in the second half of an exercise book, after samples of assorted legal forms and some poems.

Several of the rules cautioned against Seneca's bête noire, anger. ". . . in reproving show no signs of cholor but do it with all sweetness and mildness," advised rule #45. "Be not angry at table whatever happens and if you have reason to be so, show it not . . . especially if there be strangers . . ." (rule #105). Others were rudimentary bulwarks against the grossness of life in an age when a traveler at an inn might share a bed with a stranger. "Kill no vermin, or fleas, lice, ticks, etc. in the sight of others . . ." (rule #13). "Spit not into the fire . . . nor set your feet upon the fire, especially if there be meat before it" (rule #9).

But the focus of the set was established in the very first rule. "Every action done in company ought to be done with some sign of respect to those that are present." The "Rules of Civility" are "virtues of humanity"—guidelines for dealing with others, based on attending to their situations and their sensibilities. Seneca and Addison/Cato are concerned with the inner man's peace of mind and rectitude; the "Rules" are concerned with men. "When you see a crime punished, you may be inwardly pleased; but . . . show pity to the offending sufferer" (rule #23). ". . . treat [artificers and persons of low degree] with affability and courtesy, without arrogance" (rule #36). "When a man does all he can, though it succeed not well, blame not him that did it" (rule #44). ". . . if you see any filth or thick spittle . . . upon the clothes of your companions, put it off privately" (rule #13). The decent way to behave toward criminals, craftsmen, honest failures, and people who need help varies in detail, but the principle of approach is the same.

Washington bought handbooks of politeness as an adult, and instances of his courtesy, or comments on it, are legion, from Mrs. Liston, to the coughing guest at Mount Vernon who was mortified when his host appeared with a bowl of tea. His attention to civility also had political ramifications. When he gestured to Vice-President Jefferson to precede him from the dais at Adams's inauguration, he was making a political point, about the rule of law, not men. But the lesson had first been taught him as a rule of civility: "They that are in dignity or in office have in all places precedency . . ." (rule #33). Rule #32 foreshadowed later political events in a way that is almost uncanny. Nominally, it is about who gets the best bed. "To one that is your equal, or not much inferior, you are to give the chief place in your lodging, and he to whom it is offered ought at the first to refuse it, but at the second to accept though not without acknowledging his own unworthiness." The maxim begins with household arrangements, but ends by enouncing a principle of accepting honor only with reluctance and modesty, which Washington was to follow when he became Commander in Chief, president of the Constitutional Convention, and President of the United States. It is not surprising that there should have been this relation between the maxims in his exercise book and his conduct in public life, since "civility" shares the same linguistic root as "civic" and "city." The way men behave in polite society is related to how they order society. Politeness is the first form of politics.

There are as many different forms of courtesy as there are forms of society. The manners that prevailed in the English-speaking world, especially Virginia, at least until the early eighteenth century, were those of an aristocratic society, marked by sharp distinctions. Manners meant the graceful acknowledgment of others across social distances. One of the grand gestures of that system had been performed in 1704 by a Virginia gentleman, Colonel Daniel Parke, a violent and tempestuous man, who was also capable of dignity and grace. Serving in the English army, he carried the news of victory at the battle of Blenheim to Queen Anne, who offered him a reward of five hundred pounds. Parke would accept only a miniature portrait of her. Everyone in Virginia at the time knew of this gallantry; Washington may well have, since Colonel Parke was the grandfather of Daniel Parke Custis, Martha's first husband.

Aristocratic manners had an underside: those who sought attention across the social gap, whether for themselves or for some project, had to resort to flattery and hypocrisy to attract royal or noble eyes. Washington certainly knew this, from his own experience in the French and Indian War. In 1757, he tried to press a scheme for frontier defense on the British commander in chief in North America, John Campbell, fourth earl of Loudon. The mode of flattery he employed was to deny that that was what he was doing. "Do not think, my Lord, that I am going to flatter; notwithstanding I have exalted sentiments of your Lordship's character and respect your rank, it is not my intention to adulate. My nature is open and honest and free from guile!"[11] The exclamation point underlines the insincerity. (Lord Loudon rejected the advice.)

All modern manners in the western world were originally aristocratic. "Courtesy" meant behavior appropriate to a court; "chivalry" comes from "chevalier"—a knight. Yet Washington was to dedicate himself to freeing America from a court's control. Could manners survive the operation? A year and a half into Washington's presidency, Edmund Burke, reacting to the first insults offered the King and Queen of France by that revolution, argued that they could not. "The age of chivalry is gone," he keened. "Never, never more, shall we behold that generous loyalty to rank and sex, that proud submission, that dignified obedience, that subordination of the heart, which kept alive, even in servitude itself, the spirit of an exalted freedom."[12] According to Burke, the only alternative to the proud submission of a Colonel Parke, and the less-than-proud submission of a Colonel Washington, was a society cobbled together by force and self-interest.

The "Rules of Civility" suggested a third option. Without realizing it, the Jesuits who wrote them, and the young man who copied them, were outlining and absorbing a system of courtesy appropriate to equals and near-equals. "To one that is your equal, or not much your inferior . . ." begins the pantomime about the best bed, which was to be reenacted in Philadelphia and New York almost two hundred years later. When the company for whom decent behavior was to be performed expanded to the nation, Washington was ready. Parson Weems got this right, when he wrote that it was "no wonder every body honoured him who honoured every body."[13]

Washington's morality enjoined him to be courteous; he was goaded to good behavior, and to doing well, by concern for his reputation.

Washington and his contemporaries thought of reputation as a thing that might be destroyed or sullied—some valuable cargo carried in the hold of the self. When Knox wrote Lafayette that Washington, in going to the Constitutional Convention, had "committed" his fame "to the mercy of events," they were like two merchants discussing the risky venture of a third. The cargo was precious because reputation was held to be a true measure of one's character—indeed, in some sense, identical to it. We worry about our authenticity— about whether our presentation reflects who we "really" are. Eighteenth-century Americans attended more to the outside story and were less avid to drive putty knives between the outer and inner man. "Character," as Forrest McDonald has explained, was a role one played until one became it; "character" also meant how one's role was judged by others.[14] It was both the performance and the reviews. Every man had a character to maintain; every man was a character actor.

When Washington was appointed Commander in Chief, he explained his acceptance of the job to Martha in exactly these terms. "My Dearest . . . It was utterly out of my power to refuse this appointment, without exposing my character to such censures, as would have reflected dishonor upon myself, and given pain to my friends. This, I am sure, could not, and ought not, to be pleasing to you, and must have lessened me considerably in my own esteem."[15] Washington wanted the job; he had come to Congress wearing his twenty-year-old uniform, by way of dropping a visual hint. But he wanted even more not to fail to do something he ought to do.

Defeat posed a lesser threat to his reputation than dishonor. It was bad enough to lose the Battle of Long Island; far worse to flee from Kip's Bay without making a stand. Two weeks after that debacle, Washington wrote his cousin from Harlem that he faced "the impossibility of serving with reputation," on account of the militia's incompetence. He warned his cousin not to mention his fears to anyone yet, but added that "if I fall," the military circumstances should be publicized, "in credit to the justice of my character."[16] Losing or dying could be extenuated, could, in the right circumstances, be heroic. But dishonor was an inexpungeable blot.

At war's end, Washington's reputation, swollen to enormous proportions, made him invaluable to the supporters of the Constitution and a bane to its enemies. It also made his support of the Constitution a matter of enormous delicacy to him. When he had surrendered his commission in 1783, he had told

Congress that it was the "last solemn act of my Official life." He could only return to official life in 1787 if he could be sure that in doing so he was seen to bow to political necessity. "[I]nform me confidentially what the public expectation is on this head," he wrote Knox two months before the Convention, "that is, whether I will, or ought to be there?" Similar concerns attended his decision to accept the presidency both the first and the second time. Even an act as straightforward as giving a farewell address, he wrote Madison in 1792, "may be construed into a manoeuvre to be invited to remain."[17] There were potential pitfalls wherever the scrupulous bearer of a reputation stepped—none more treacherous than the one pointed out to him by Mrs. Powel: that he might acquire a reputation for being obsessed with his reputation. Washington wished to succeed in office, but he needed to avoid dishonor in pursuing it.

Countries, like individuals, have reputations, and Washington was as concerned for America's as he was for his own. "We have now a National character to establish," he wrote, three weeks after addressing the officers at Newburgh, "and it is of the utmost importance to stamp favorable impressions upon it." One way a country did this was by sound finances. Washington had a Virginia planter's horror of debt, made more acute by the fact that so many planters slid insensibly into it and compounded by his experience as Commander of an ill-paid army. In one of his last letters to Jefferson, in a list of villainous types, he ranked defaulters and pickpockets behind the emperor Nero. Though the word "credit" now has an almost entirely financial meaning, it is related to reputation. Sound money is reputable money. Another way of establishing national character, Washington believed, was by avoiding weakness and disunity. Shays' Rebellion had plunged "this rising empire in wretchedness and contempt;" the Whiskey Rebellion had risked the country's "reputation and strength."[18] But as with individuals, energy and strength had to be directed to just ends. A government that was strong but tyrannical could have no better reputation than Nero or a defaulter.

The reputations of nations and individuals could reinforce each other, particularly if the individual had founded the nation. In the midst of the struggle to ratify the Constitution, Washington wrote Lafayette one of the few letters in his vast output that is unconsciously revealing—in which the putty knife finds a crack. The text is the reputation of great men; the subtext is his own. After some introductory courtesies, Washington recommends to Lafayette's attention Joel Barlow, a recent emigrant to Paris. Barlow was a typical American of a certain kind, half polymath and half fraud, who had tried his hand at the ministry, journalism, the law, land speculation, and poetry. In this last capacity, Barlow had written a patriotic epic, the *Vision of Columbus.* "Mr. Barlow," wrote Washington, "is considered by those who are good Judges to be a genius of the first magnitude. . . ." Such is the misplaced pride of little countries. American political philosophy was great; some of its painters were good. But as a poet, Mr. Barlow was not a genius of the first or any magnitude, as these lines on American riflemen show:

[They]
Cull out the distant foe in full horse speed,
Couch the long tube and eye the silver bead,
Turn as he turns, dismiss the whizzing lead,
And lodge the death-ball in his heedless head.

"Heedless head" is more lethal than any bullet.

But Washington had something more than literary criticism in mind when he wrote to Lafayette. For Barlow, he went on, was "one of those Bards who hold the keys of the gate by which Patriots, Sages and Heroes are admitted to immortality. Such are your Antient Bards who are both the priest and doorkeepers to the temple of fame. And these, my dear Marquis, are no vulgar functions." For this reason, great men throughout history have supplied poets with patronage as well as subject matter. "In some instances by acting reciprocally, heroes have made poets, and poets heroes." Washington proceeded to offer examples: Alexander ("said to have been enraptured with the Poems of Homer, and to have lamented that he had not a rival muse to celebrate his actions"); Caesar ("well known to have been a man of a highly cultivated understanding and taste"); Augustus ("the professed and magnificent rewarder of poetical merit, nor did he lose the return of having his atchievments immortalized in song"). "Perhaps," he added, getting warmer, "we shall be found, at this moment, not inferior to the rest of the world in the performances of our poets and painters. . . ." Then, feeling the heat, he turned abruptly away. "I hardly know how it is that I am drawn thus far in observations on a subject so foreign from those in which we are mostly engaged, farming and politics, unless because I had little news to tell you." He went on, notwithstanding, to tell some important news: the Constitution had been ratified by eight states, and Virginia, the ninth, would begin its debates the following week, for which Washington held out "good hopes. . . . The plot thickens fast."[19] And if the plot succeeded, Washington did not add, Barlow and his fellow bards would have a plot indeed. Washington could not tell even Lafayette—he could not tell himself—that he hoped his reputation would be honored in later years by the country he had made and celebrated by its poets. But he did hope it.

Washington managed to attract talents greater than Barlow's, during his life and after his death, for Trumbull painted him, and John Marshall and Washington Irving—one of the many children named after him—wrote biographies of him. Walt Whitman wrote a short poem, "The Centenarian's Story," about a blind old man, at a parade of Civil War recruits in Brooklyn, remembering the Battle of Long Island, eighty-five years earlier: the British attack, the night crossing of the East River, the dismay.

> Every one else seem'd fill'd with gloom,
> Many no doubt thought of capitulation.

> But when my General pass'd me,
> As he stood in his boat and look'd toward the coming sun,
> I saw something different from capitulation.[20]

It is a good editorial in free verse—a hundred times better than "heedless head."

Was this enough? We are now in an age when statesmen cannot write, and writers and painters view statesmen with contempt, perhaps with reason. But even before the modern divorce of arts and deeds, no one did for Washington what Augustus Saint-Gaudens did for Farragut, Sherman, or Colonel Robert Shaw, or what Whitman did for Lincoln. He has been disappointed in his hopes.

Courtesy and reputation—the medium and the stimulus of Washington's morality—operate on and through other people. Courtesy is how you treat them, reputation is what they think of you. The result of Washington's lifelong concern with courtesy and reputation was that he was able to put the strenuous morals of the noble Romans in a social context and make *Cato*'s best lines real. " 'Tis not in mortals to command success,/ But *we'll* do more, Sempronius, *we'll* deserve it." How could deserving Romans justify the plural? On Addison's own showing, the most deserving Roman of them all affected nothing outside his little band and died by his own hand. Courtesy and reputation made it possible for a would-be Roman in the North American boondocks to say to his countrymen, *we*, and to command a response.

IDEAS

We think of Washington as badly educated for two reasons: he thought so, and many of the people around him thought so.

After the war, Washington encouraged David Humphreys, a former aide, to write a biography of him, since his own "consciousness of a defective education" prevented him from setting down his memoirs. (Humphreys pottered at the task for some years without finishing it; ironically, the best parts of the false start are some brief descriptions of episodes from the French and Indian War, supplied by Washington himself.) "His time was employed in action chiefly," recalled Jefferson, "reading little, and that only in agriculture and English history." Adams recalled Washington's level of education even more acidly: "he was too illiterate, unlearned, unread for his station and reputation. . . ."[1]

All of these colleagues had been to college: Humphreys to Yale, Jefferson to William and Mary, Adams to Harvard. Many of the founding elite, especially among the younger generation, had college educations. Twenty-four of the delegates to the Constitutional Convention had been to college, nine of them to the College of New Jersey at Princeton. Hamilton had applied to go there, but the school would not let him study at his own pace, so he went to King's (later Columbia) instead. Aaron Burr made it through Princeton without difficulty. Franklin never went to college, but he compensated by founding one (Pennsylvania).

We know almost nothing about Washington's schooling, and there can't be much to know. His father hired a tutor, and he also attended a country school. His schooling was over by age fifteen. No other President, except Andrew Johnson, had so little formal training. Washington's education was the equivalent of grade school, plus instruction in surveying. By the time he was sixteen, he was practicing his skill.

Yet Washington was self-evidently intelligent, informed, and judicious. Biographers bridge the gap between the meager foundation and the impressive structure by making much of his "education" by other means—in life, from experience on the frontier. He had all that, as any man (even an intellectual) must, if he hopes to have an effect on the world. But vague talk of learning by doing underestimates the importance to Washington of right ideas—the third story of his character. It was in the name of right ideas about politics and government that he commanded his countrymen, and the process of studying them, and sharpening his understanding of them, went on all his adult life.

Machiavelli made a famous division of rulers into three categories—those smart enough to figure things out by themselves, those smart enough to understand the explanations of others, those too stupid to do either. The distinctions are useful, though Machiavelli's analysis is an uneasy mixture of job application (hire me, and learn the secrets of statecraft) and condescension toward those to be taught (which may explain why he was rarely hired). Washington was a leader who sought explanations and explainers all his life, and who mastered both what he was told and those who told him.

He sought political ideas, in the first place, by reading. Washington had, at his death, a library of nine hundred volumes, and despite Jefferson's comments, many authors besides agriculturalists and historians were represented in it, including Jefferson himself. For almost forty years, Washington kept up with the controversial political literature of North America at a time when it was of the highest order. He had had a sporting interest in politics since he was a teenager, when his half-brother Lawrence was reelected to the House of Burgesses, and George saved the tally of voters. His own career in the House coincided with an era of constitutional pamphleteering, in which he immersed himself, even as he played a role in the constitutional struggles. If he had not mastered the pamphlets, he would not have played the role he did. Washington had bad personal experiences with Britons and British institutions throughout the 1750s and 1760s: During the French and Indian War, he was forced, as an officer in the militia, to serve on a lower footing than officers of the same rank in the regular army; as a peacetime tobacco grower, he depended for all his luxuries and many of his necessities on his London agents, or factors, who acted as buyers, suppliers, and bankers all in one—a relationship rife with opportunities for misunderstandings and ill feeling. Still, it was reading that gave these discontents direction.

The first fight of his political career was the Parson's Cause, a struggle in 1760 over who would control the salaries of Anglican clergymen in Virginia. Washington followed the pamphlet wars provoked by it and by every subsequent struggle of the next fourteen years. He bought his first Jefferson, "A Summary View of the Rights of British America," the warm-up for the Declaration, as he was leaving for the First Continental Congress. The process was repeated after the war. Though Washington's experience as Commander in Chief disposed him to a stronger national government, reading showed him the way. During the debate over the constitution, he read, besides the *Federalist,* the essays of half a dozen other polemicists, pro and con, and he cited this "long and laborious investigation" in his discarded first Inaugural Address. Despite his sensitivity to the rascally Freneau, Washington as President repeatedly urged that newspapers be carried free of charge; a visitor to Mount Vernon in his final retirement noted that he still took ten newspapers.

Whenever possible, he talked to the authors he read; often, they wrote for him. In the decade before the revolution, the role had been filled by his neighbor George Mason. Madison served as intellectual mentor from the mid-1780s until the end of his first term, with Hamilton sharing and then taking over the role. Washington knew when to take on an intellectual guide. But when he and a pathfinder disagreed, he found another. The fact that he had several over the course of his political career suggests that he was in thrall to none of them. Hamilton defined the relationship, for himself and for all would-be Machiavellis, when he wrote, after Washington's death, that the ex-President had been "an *Aegis very essential to me.*"[2] The aegis was the shield of Zeus, who loaned it to Athena and Apollo, the intellectuals of Olympus, but never gave it away.

An indication of the importance Washington attached to ideas was his stubborn advocacy of a national university, to be located in the as-yet-unbuilt capital. This was the one policy prescription of his that never bore fruit. Even his vision of an east-west canal became real, in New York, if not Virginia. The national university went nowhere, and yet he pushed for it throughout the last decade of his life. He mentioned the idea in his annual messages to Congress and at the end of his second term, he considered importing the faculty of the university of Geneva to the Potomac to do the job. Students, he wrote Jefferson, could attend the debates in Congress and study republican virtue. (He assumed there would be a connection.)[3] Washington did not want learning for its own sake, but political education in the principles and practice of self-government: the same kind of education he had given himself.

Washington's understanding of self-government rested on his understanding of human nature, which he had formed before the Revolution. In 1769, he wrote Mason about the importance of "maintain[ing] the liberty which we have derived from our Ancestors."[4] This was the radical as conservative—a description that fit almost all Americans of the patriot party, who resented Parliament and the king as innovators seeking to impose on a patchwork, live-and-let-live empire a newfangled system run out of London. Washington moved toward rebellion because he believed his rights as an Englishman, which had been transformed by immigration and generations of residence into the rights of a Virginian, were being trampled upon by the imperial center. But at the same time, he conceived of his rights in universal terms. This was the conservative as radical, defending old customs and privileges because he was entitled to them as a man.

In 1774, he wrote a political letter to Bryan Fairfax, son of his old mentor William. Washington had taken command of the Fairfax County militia, but the county's namesake was feeling the reservations of a Tory. Washington began by saying that he had no "arguments to offer in support of my own doctrine," beyond those which already filled the papers. He outlined two.

". . . an innate spirit of freedom, first told me that [Parliament's] measures . . . are repugnant to every principle of natural justice; whilst much abler heads than my own hath fully convinced me that" they are "subversive of the laws and constitution of Great Britain itself . . ."[5] Washington appealed to both the laws of Britain and the laws of nature; "abler heads" (Mason's?) had to untangle the mazes and precedents of British justice, but he could figure out natural justice himself.

Washington's ideas about the principles of natural justice were not unique to him. Like the kindred sentiments of the Declaration of Independence, they were platitudes—"expression[s] of the American mind," as Jefferson put it. They were everywhere; they were in the air. They had filled many pages of polemic and exposition and many hours of sermons, oratory, and talk. They were visible in nature itself. "The sacred rights of mankind," wrote Hamilton, ". . . are written, as with a sunbeam, in the whole *volume* of human nature, by the hand of the Divinity itself. . . ."[6] They underlay all Washington's later wrestling, as President, with the problems of self-government. His notions of the respect people owed the excise laws, or the respect the government owed its own treaties, assumed a government that had been justly founded. If the United States were not grounded in right ideas, then he, and everyone who supported him, were simply carving for themselves.

Neither Washington's ideas, nor his belief that right ideas were a necessary attainment of public men, have survived in their original form. We take his vision of a national university even less seriously than his contemporaries did, for while the federal government spends billions of dollars on higher education and shapes its direction with a heavy hand, it is interested chiefly in scientific research, in theories and techniques that might benefit the economy or the military. Otherwise, academics are left free to pursue what interests them. The only people interested in instilling a theory of public order through public education are the apostles of diversity, and their program has less to do with human rights than with a systematic carving for one's group. Conservatives, who profess loyalty to the intentions of the founders, have such a deep suspicion of the intentions of modern educators that most of them want the public education establishment broken up. And who, considering what educators teach and students learn, can blame them?

Politicians pay equally slight attention to political theory, despite occasional tags of convention rhetoric, bleached to bone dryness. When Newt Gingrich became Speaker of the House, he actually made news by suggesting that freshmen congressmen should read the Declaration of Independence, the *Federalist,* and *Democracy in America* (as well as a biography of Washington). But he muddied his own recommendation by adding tracts on computers, corporate management, and futurism to his reading list. It is as if Gingrich wanted the congressmen to emulate Jefferson's slighting and inaccurate memory of Washington's reading. The computer and business literature could stand in for agriculture, while Alvin and Heidi Toffler, Gingrich's futurists, seem to stand in for English history, though what the Tofflers really offer is trendology—analyzing past eras, so as to master the next one. There was equivalent stuff available during the Washington administration: the Marquis de Condorcet, a French mathematician and friend of Jefferson, wrote an outline of the ten ages of history before committing suicide to avoid the guillotine in 1794. But Washington did not waste any time on him.

Washington's political ideas have fared worse at our hands than his image did at John Trumbull's.

* * *

Besides the literature of American political theory, Washington was influenced by two coherent systems of thought—Christianity and Freemasonry.

No aspect of his life has been more distorted than his religion. Washington was born an Anglican, like most Virginians of his time and class, and served on the vestry of his parish church. When the church in America reconstituted itself as Episcopalian after the Revolution, he went along with it. After his first inaugural, he walked to a service at St. Paul's Chapel on Broadway, which still identifies his pew. The rector of Christ Church and St. Peter's in Philadelphia described him as "serious and attentive" at services, though he seems not to have taken communion (Martha invariably did).[7]

But what did his affiliation mean? For two centuries, Washington has been a screen on which Americans have projected their religious wishes and aversions. For the first hundred years after his death, it was fashionable to make him pious. The most famous legend of his devotion is the story of him praying in the snow at Valley Forge, but there are many others, some quite arcane. The Shakers claimed to have communicated with his spirit. Catholic magazines, until fairly recently, still reprinted the supposed reminiscences of an old soldier who testified that the Commander's prayers at Valley Forge had been answered by an apparition of the Virgin Mary.

For the last hundred years, the fashion, among scholars at least, has run the other way. In "The Young Man Washington," Samuel Eliot Morison declared that he had "found no trace of Biblical phraseology" in Washington's letters. If Morison meant that Washington never wrote in the style of the Bible, he was right, though who in the eighteenth century did? If he meant that Washington never quoted Biblical phrases, he was simply wrong. Morison's failure to find them is all the more strange since he argues that young Washington was influenced by Marcus Aurelius, of whom it can be said that there is no trace in Washington's letters or his library. More recently, Paul K. Longmore, while acknowledging "occasional references" to scripture in Washington's writing, says that they "evidence no deep study." No deep study of theology, perhaps, although several of Washington's Biblical allusions are put to deep uses.[8]

Washington's most famous utterance on religion is probably the paragraph from his Farewell Address, which begins, "Of all the dispositions and habits which lead to political prosperity, Religion and morality are indispensable supports. In vain would that man claim the tribute of Patriotism, who should labour to subvert these great Pillars of human happiness, these firmest props of the duties of Men and citizens. The mere Politician, equally with the pious man, ought to respect and cherish them. . . ." This cool, utilitarian analysis certainly sounds like the work of a politician, rather than a pious man. "Supports," "Pillars," "props" are the language of a building inspector. Washington's General Orders, in the early days of the war, urging "punctual attendance on divine Service," in a paragraph forbidding swearing and drunkenness, are of the same tendency. They support the impression of an eighteenth-century squire, serving as a vestryman and attending church because it was what one did and seeing that others did it too. When he moved from the manor house to the presidential mansion, the squire broadened his rhetoric accordingly, writing to Jews in Savannah who had congratulated him on his election of "Jehovah," speaking to a delegation of Cherokees of the "Great spirit," and attending a Dutch Reformed service, "which, being in the language not a word of which I understood, I was in no danger of becoming a proselyte . . ."[9]

If these had been the sum of his attitudes and opinions, Washington was in no danger of becoming a proselyte in any language. But he had a warm and lively belief, repeatedly expressed in private and in public, in Providence. Washington's God was no watchmaker, who wound the world up and retired, but an active agent and force. This conviction may have been instilled in him by the experience of Braddock's defeat. The young man who had been charmed by the bullet's whistle was not charmed when several bullets whistled through his coat, and he saw death and destruction on every side. "See the wondrous works of Providence!" he wrote afterward. "The uncertainty of human things!"[10]

Providence could also do enormous good and deserved thanks when He, or It, did. The Battle of Monmouth would have been lost, Washington wrote one of his brothers, but for "that bountiful Providence which has never failed us in the hour of distress. . . ." The General Orders after Yorktown called for divine services to recognize the "reiterated and astonishing interpositions of Providence. . . ." He devoted a third of his first Inaugural Address to a discussion of the "providential agency" at work in the founding—"reflections [which] have forced themselves too strongly on my mind to be suppressed." ". . . as the allwise disposer of events has hitherto watched over my steps," he wrote while deciding whether to serve a second term, "I trust that in the important one I may soon be called upon to take, he will mark the course so plainly . . . that [I] cannot mistake the way." In one letter, after one of these descants, he made something like a joke. ". . . it will be time enough for me to turn preacher when my present appointment ceases, and therefore I shall add no more on the Doctrine of Providence."[11] But this is not a joke about the all-disposing power or about belief in it, but about his own capacities to talk about it. Sometimes there are things too great to praise. Washington drew the veil.

Providence can be conceived in many ways, not necessarily

Christian. The Biblical allusions that Morison missed show Washington making use of Christian conceptions and beliefs, in novel ways.

His favorite scriptural phrase was from a description of the reign of Solomon (I Kings 4:25): "Judah and Israel dwelt safely, every man under his vine and under his fig tree." Washington used the vine and fig tree mostly as a tag, to describe retirement at Mount Vernon. But in one letter, the tag gained a dimension of nobility. Religious congregations of all kinds sent Washington greetings and memorials throughout his presidency, to which he responded with public pronouncements. His answer to the Hebrew Congregation of Newport is justly celebrated for its statement that the government of the United States "gives to bigotry no sanctions, to persecution no assistance. . . ." The conclusion cast the message into poetry, no less moving for being borrowed: "every one shall sit in safety under his own vine and fig tree and there shall be none to make him afraid."[12]

Washington's postwar sale's pitch to Lafayette, boosting the Ohio Valley with a trio of Biblical allusions, opened with yet another: that settling the West would fulfill "the first and greatest commandment, *Increase and Multiply.*"[13] "Be fruitful and multiply" is the first commandment to humans in the Bible, for it is what God tells Adam and Eve in the Garden. But it is odd to call it the "greatest" commandment: what about "Thou shalt have no other gods before me," the first of the Ten Commandments; or "Thou shalt love the Lord thy God with all thy heart, and with all thy soul, and with all thy mind" (which Jesus called the "first and great commandment")? For all his joshing tone—Washington knows he is laying it on thick for Lafayette's benefit—he writes of settlers as if they were before or beyond formal worship, moving into Eden.

There is no joshing in the quotation that ends Washington's

Circular to the States, a formal message to the thirteen governors that the Commander in Chief issued in June 1783, six months before resigning. The Circular was Washington's first Farewell Address, a political last will and testament. Though it is less comprehensive than the more famous Farewell, the prose is statelier and more compact, perhaps because Hamilton had no hand in writing it. It ends with an "earnest prayer," based on Micah 6:8, which instructs Israel how to behave. ". . . what doth the LORD require of thee, but to do justly, and to love mercy, and to walk humbly with thy God?" The Commander in Chief hoped Americans would "do Justice . . . love mercy, and . . . demean ourselves with that Charity, humility and pacific temper of mind, which were the Characteristicks of the Divine Author of our blessed Religion, and without an humble imitation of whose example in these things, we can never hope to be a happy Nation." Washington raised the ante of the last phrase immeasurably: Americans should not just be humble, but show the humility of Christ (one of the few references to Christ he ever made).

But the prayer of the Circular, like the other Biblical allusions, also deflects the Bible into politics. Americans should not walk "with" God, but apply His Son's "characteristicks" to their relations with each other. Politics takes on the functions of religion: the government shall rule like Solomon; the people will populate Eden and imitate Christ. Lincoln is the premier American bender of the Bible to political purposes. He was a greater stylist than Washington, with the cadences of the King James Version in his lungs. But in this, as in so many other ways, Lincoln followed where the founders led.

Believers must be suspicious of such borrowings, for they can easily slip into blasphemy. Yet men must live in society, and unless a believer is a hermit, God's injunctions to Israel or Jesus' to the disciples will be of some relevance to social organization. Without giving bigotry any sanctions, Washington sought to borrow what was useful in Christianity for the United States.

Washington belonged to another religious body besides the Episcopal Church—the Freemasons. Washington's Freemasonry is a difficult subject, not because everyone cares about it, but because hardly anyone does. The only people interested in Freemasonry are Masons and anti-Masons; almost everything written about it is either self-infatuated or loony, in the manner of the teenage pothead in the movie *Dazed and Confused*. "The founding fathers belonged to a cult, man. . . . There's spooky stuff on the back of a dollar bill." (He was right about the dollar bill; that odd little pyramid surmounted by an unwinking eyeball is Masonic iconography, suggested by Benjamin Franklin, who published the *Constitutions* of Masonry in Philadelphia in 1734.)

Washington became a Mason in his early twenties. Most biographers follow Morison's explanation, that he did it because he was a "good 'joiner.' "[14] Maybe so; but in 1793, when Washington laid the cornerstone of the Capitol, Lodge 22 of Alexandria organized the parade, with Washington serving as Grand Master *pro tem* and wearing a Masonic apron knitted for him by Madame Lafayette, whose husband belonged to the lodge of Saint-Jean de la Candeur. This would seem to go beyond the requirements of "joining."

What could Masonry have meant to him? Modern Freemasonry, despite many fanciful claims to antiquity, was invented in London in 1717, when a group of intellectuals, many of them fellows of the Royal Society, took over a craft guild and turned it into a secret society dedicated to enlightened uplift. They believed in God, but in a way that tended to shuck off traditional Christian forms. The newcomers elaborated a new mythology and ritual to express their worldview. The legend of the Third Degree of Masonry took off from a Biblical account of Huram, King of Tyre, who sent Solomon a "cunning man," also named Huram, "skilful to work" on the Temple (II Chronicles 2:13–14). In the Masonic version, the cunning man is killed by workers to whom he would not reveal the Master Word of his craft. When Solomon asked other masons to find him, they agreed that if the master was dead, the first word they spoke when they found his body should become the new Master Word.[15] The story seems to teach, among other things, getting the job done by new means if the old have failed or vanished.

In Europe, Freemasonry was anticlerical, and the Catholic Church anti-Masonic. (The church would rightly see itself as the Old Word.) In the United States, Freemasonry was assailed as irreligious and revolutionary in the late 1790s by Congregationalist divines, the religious right of that day. Thirty years later, a second outbreak of anti-Masonry attacked its rituals as unrepublican and even formed a political party to crusade against the menace. The issue has not died yet; in 1992, Pat Robertson published a book accusing Freemasons of pulling the strings of the Bush administration, world communism, and other sinister organizations. American anti-Masons have always had to climb over the fact of Washington's membership. The Yankee preachers, Federalists all, distinguished between ordinary Masons (good) and "illuminated" Masons (very bad), while the Anti-Masonic Party took the tack that Washington hadn't been told what was going on; to think anything else, declared William Wirt, the party's presidential candidate, "would be parricide."[16]

The difficulty with assessing the intellectual effect of Freemasonry on Washington is that it is redundant, as far as its content is concerned. It is not clear what content it had in America. Masons were found among American revolutionaries and Tories alike. In pre-Revolutionary Boston, Americans in colonial government and the Anglican church belonged to one lodge; Paul Revere and John Hancock belonged to another. The impulse to extract what was useful from Christianity was also not unique to Masons. Jefferson, who compiled his own stripped-down version of the Gospels, was not a Freemason.

Masonry, in the English-speaking world of Washington's day, was the mumbo-jumbo of the Enlightenment. Christianity makes good use of mumbo-jumbo; believers think there is more to its sacraments than that, but there is also that to them. Why shouldn't the enlightened make use of it too? To a man enamored of drama as Washington was, Freemasonry gave symbolic and ceremonial form to goals and ideas he already had. When it came time to lay the cornerstone of the republic's temple, what better rites to use than those supposedly descended from Solomon's architect?

Washington also gratified his taste for the dramatic by attending plays. The theater was the final component of his intellectual being, and what was most important to him was not the message of any particular play, but the experience of playgoing and the shape of dramatic performance.

A night at the theater was then a more expansive and variegated experience than it is now. Actors took liberties with even the most popular plays. The English actor David Garrick rewrote speeches from *Richard III*, his greatest role; *King Lear* was typically performed with a happy ending (Dr. Johnson said he could not bear to reread the tragic original). Theater in America was conducted along the same lines: a grand hodgepodge, with interpolations and star turns. The bill for one performance that President Washington attended, with the Chief Justice and the Secretary of War, gives the flavor:

An **Opera**, or, Dramatic Romance, called,

CYMON and SYLVIA,

or, *Love and Magic.*

With a Grand Procession of Knights of the different orders of chivalry, shepherds and shepherdesses of Arcadia, Cymon and Sylvia in a Triumphal Car, *&c, &c.*

In Act 5th, will be introduced the original scene of the

SINKING of the *BLACK TOWER,*

End of the 4th Act, Hippesly's *Drunken Man,*

By **Mr. Henry,**

End of the Play, (by particular desire,) the second time,

A MONODY,

Or, Eulogium on the American Chief who fell in the

Cause of Freedom.

To make mankind in conscious virtue bold,
Live o'er each scene, and be what they behold.—Pope

The Recitation and vocal parts, (as the *Genius of Columbia*)

By **Mrs. Henry.**

To which will be added, a Comedy, in two Acts. . . .[17]

Washington saw his first play—George Lillo's *The London Merchant*, a weeper about the corruption of an apprentice—on his only trip abroad, when he accompanied his ailing half-brother to Barbados. Thereafter, whenever business took him to Williamsburg or some larger town, he saw whatever was available. During the French and Indian War, while passing through New York, he twice viewed "The Microcosm," an elaborate contraption that was a cross between a diorama and a music box, which displayed the planets, the Muses, Orpheus, carpenters at work, singing birds, and sailing ships, "in a very elegant Manner." He was not content merely to quote *Cato*, but had it performed at Valley Forge. "The scenery was in Taste—& the performance admirable," wrote Colonel William Bradford, one of the officers who was in the audience. "Col. George," one of the officers in the cast, "did his part to admiration—he made an excellent die (as they say)—Pray heaven, he dont die in earnest—for yesterday he was seized with the pleurisy. . . ." Washington saw Shakespeare several times in his life, though in productions that would strike us as offbeat. During the Constitutional Convention, he caught John Dryden's modernization of *The Tempest*, with music by Henry Purcell, while during his first term, there was a children's performance of *Julius Caesar* in the presidential mansion, with George Custis in the role of Cassius. Sometimes Washington was the subject of the pieces he saw. One program he attended with the French minister, which included a comedy in French, a farce, and "several curious dances," ended with a display of "thirteen pyramidal pillars, representing the thirteen States—on the middle column was seen a Cupid, supporting a laurel crown over the motto—WASHINGTON—the pride of his country and terror of Britain. . . . The spectacle ended with an artificial illumination of the thirteen columns." Washington never acted on stage himself, but his appearances were studied professionally. The manager of Ricketts' Circus in Philadelphia told George Custis that he made a point of observing the President "when I hear that he is abroad on horseback; his seat is so firm, his management so easy and graceful, that I, who am a [teacher] of horsemanship, would go to him and learn to ride."[18]

There were periods when Washington's love of the theater ran counter to political fashion. In the fall of 1778, only five months after the Valley Forge production of *Cato*, Congress resolved that "whereas true religion and good morals are the only solid foundations of public liberty and happiness," plays "and such other diversions as are productive of idleness, dissipation, and a general depravity of principles and manners" be suppressed. (The French minister explained the law to his government thus: "It is the northern members, called the Presbyterian party, that delight in passing moral laws. . . .") During his presidency, Washington invited the prickly Senator Maclay of Pennsylvania to be his guest at a production of Richard Brinsley Sheridan's *The School for Scandal*. "I never liked" the play, wrote Maclay in his diary. "Indeed, I think it an indecent representation before ladies of character and virtue."[19]

Washington quoted from *Cato*, occasionally from Shakespeare. But more often, his letters and addresses alluded to the theater itself, to acting and stages and dramas, using its terms to describe the tasks facing his country, himself, or his fellows. "We are placed among the Nations of the Earth, and have a character to establish," he wrote Lafayette in April 1783, as his tenure as Commander in Chief was coming to a close. ". . . we shall be guilty of many blunders in treading this boundless theatre before we have arrived at any perfection in this Art." He employed the same metaphor two weeks later in his General Orders to the soon-to-be-disbanded army. "Nothing now remains but for the actors of this mighty Scene to preserve a perfect, unvarying consistency of character through the very last act; to close the Drama with applause; and to retire from the Military Theatre with the same approbation of Angells and men which have crowned all their former vertuous Actions."[20] Playacting and playgoing reinforced the notion of reputation as a character to be maintained by right actions.

The other lesson that Washington took from the theater was that all plays end, and all actors make exits. This bore directly on his performance as a military and political actor. The political theory of the day taught the same lesson; Americans threw off a king so as to have rulers who would be held responsible to the people by elections or, in some cases, made subservient to them by "rotation"—what is now called term limits. In the spring of 1775 Washington's friend George Mason made a learned argument for rotation as the principle of service for officers in the Fairfax County militia. He began by invoking Machiavelli—not the counselor to despots, but the author of the republican *Discourses* (Machiavelli was nothing if not versatile). "[T]he deepest politician who ever put pen to paper" had written "that no institution can be long preserved, but by frequent recurrence to those maxims on which it was founded." What maxims, Mason asked, were appropriate to a popular militia? ". . . whenever any military establishment or authority is not, by some certain mode of rotation, dissolved into and blended with that mass from which it was taken, inevitable destruction to the state follows." One-year terms would "prevent abuse of authority, and the insolence of office. . . ." But Mason made an exception for one officer, the company commander, Colonel Washington—"a very proper one, justly due to his public merit and experience," and "dictated, not by compliment, but conviction."[21] Theorists can always spin an exception, find the loophole. Mason was a scrupulously honorable man, as his conduct at the Constitutional Convention would show. But even honorable men can crack the door for dishonor if they think too long. In other circumstances, for other men, Mason's exception might have been the seed of American *caudillismo*. By supplementing his reading in theory with his experience of the stage, where the lights go out on everyone, with no exceptions, Washington had armored himself doubly against such a possibility. Though he did accept reelection as commander of the Fairfax militia, he closed the dramas of Commander in Chief and President by his own exit.

So it was appropriate that on his last day as President, when he wrote Jonathan Trumbull, brother of the painter and governor of Connecticut, he employed a theatrical metaphor: ". . . the curtain drops on my political life . . . this evening, I expect for ever. . . ."[22]

If there was one aspect of Washington's character that was more important than the other two, it was his concern for civility and reputation, which tamed and smoothed his natural endowments and brought his ideas into daily life. Morals integrated him and held his being together, even as they connected him with his fellow Americans. Each aspect was necessary, however. Without his physique and the threat of his temper, he would have been inconsiderable; without his ideas, he might have been passive and directionless. If he had lacked any of the three or possessed any to a lesser degree, he could not have been the father of his country.

Founding Father

FATHERS

We speak of "founding fathers," in the plural. Yet there has only been one "father" of this country. National paternity began gravitating to Washington six months before the Declaration of Independence, when one Levi Allen addressed him in a letter as "our political Father." The first reference to him as "Father of His country" appeared in an almanac in 1778, and since then the title has been fixed.[1]

That title is the greatest barrier to our appreciation of him now, for never was the comparative term of the metaphor so problematic. We are not sure what the fathers of families do, much less fathers of countries. The stereotype father of the fifties, who worked till five then read the paper, has been replaced by a new stereotype of dad as diaper changer. But the increased role taken by fathers in rearing children (by those who actually take the role rather than just talk about it) has been more than offset by the increased number of fathers who have disappeared through the escape hatch of divorce. Joint custody is an inadequate recompense. Other fathers vanish preemptively, by not marrying the mothers of their children in the first place, while the men who take their places—stepfathers and the boyfriends of mothers—are responsible for most of the beating and raping of children that goes on. Our predicaments have a biological basis. Bearing a child takes nine months of a mother's life, and through most of that time she is in touch with what is going on inside her. She carries the weight, she feels the kicks. Once a child is born, it seems that a mother is to some degree wired to attend to it, however badly she may do the job. None of this applies to fathers. Conception is a spasm, an incident. The task can be as easily accomplished by a sperm bank or a baster. Without a blood test, fathers cannot tell how many of "their" children are their own, while mothers who have not been rigidly faithful cannot tell who are the fathers of their children.

Seneca was aware of the wispiness of literal fatherhood and wrote about it in the book Washington owned. "My father gave me the benefit of life . . . not knowing to whom, and when I was in a condition neither to feel death, nor to fear it. . . . It is true, that without a father I could never have had a being . . . but I do not, therefore, owe my virtue . . . to my nativity. . . . The generation of me was the least part of the benefit: for, to live, is common with the brutes; but, to live well is the main business. . . ."[2] If a man does only the biological minimum required for fatherhood, then he has no role in whether his children live well, or even in whether they live at all.

This is the poignance of bastardy and the irresponsibility of careless coupling. In the first scene of *King Lear*, Gloucester jokes in the presence of his bastard son Edmund. ". . . though this knave came something saucily to the world before he was sent for, yet was his mother fair, there was good sport at his making, and the whoreson must be acknowledged." He thinks he's being funny, recalling copulations past. When, an hour later, Gloucester's eyes are torn out, thanks to Edmund's plotting, we are properly appalled. But the old man had something coming, if not that.

Fatherhood, as any society understands it, is the result of training and an act of will. A man who would be a father in name as well as fact must go beyond what is merely natural. A father is a man who follows through. This is why it was particularly appropriate that Washington came to be known as the father of his country, for he was the founder, above all others, who followed through.

The old historian's parlor game, whether events make men or men make events (old because most historians long ago gave the palm to events), seldom considered the option that was always open to historical actors, which was that of doing nothing at all. If the question is, how many of Washington's public deeds were thrust upon him by circumstance, the simplest and truest answer is that none of them were, for he could always have stayed home. If an entirely private life would have been too eccentric for a man of his station—even the retiring George Mason held public office—then he could have spent his career in the planters' club of the Virginia legislature. If he had gone to the Continental Congress, he need not have taken committee chairmanships nor made himself available for military service. At the end of his tenure as Commander in Chief, he could have returned home for good and spent the remainder of his days farming and fussing with canals. If he had gone to the Constitutional Convention, he could have sent the document into the world, and not himself. After one term as President, he could have given Madison's Farewell Address. But always he did the next thing, and then the next.

The span of his accumulated follow-throughs is remarkable. Jefferson, Jackson, Wilson, Reagan, and (we now realize)

Eisenhower were strong presidents for two terms, with varying degrees of national leadership before their first elections. Franklin Roosevelt was a leader in peace and war for twelve years. Lincoln's national career lasted only seven years, from the Senate race against Stephen Douglas to his assassination. Washington was the most important man in America, whether he was onstage or off, for twenty-four years; for seventeen of those years, he was front and center. It is a record unmatched in our history, scarcely matched in the histories of modern democracies.

Washington's record as a "political Father" is all the more striking because his own father, Augustine Washington, seems to have left such a blank in his life. Augustine was thirty-eight years old when George was born, the first child of his second marriage, and he died eleven years later. We know nothing bad about Augustine Washington as a father; we also know nothing good, except for the facts that he sent his two sons by his first marriage to England to be educated, and that he left his family a substantial estate. The many volumes of Washington's collected works yield three brief references to him, all unrevealing.

Scanning Washington's life for possible father figures, one finds a few candidates. His half-brother Lawrence, fourteen years older, was a captain in the British army during a forerunner of the French and Indian War. Lawrence went off to war when George was eight; here may have begun the lifelong love of uniforms. Lawrence's marriage drew George into the land business and the penumbra of the Fairfax family. There was William Fairfax himself, mailing his young in-law maxims, and General Edward Braddock, the only British officer Washington respected, and who dealt well by him. But they do not seem to have been significant father substitutes; they do not bulk as large in Washington's life or in his recollections as he himself loomed in the lives of his protégés.

Mary Washington, George's mother, left a more vivid impression, though it is rather grim. In her later years particularly (which lasted into her son's presidency), she was stingy with praise and lavish with demands. During the Revolution, she encouraged a motion in the Virginia legislature to grant her a pension, which prompted Washington to send the Speaker of the House a mortified letter. "Before I left Virginia, I answered all her calls for money, and since that period, have directed my steward to do the same. Whence her distresses can arise, therefore, I know not . . . she has not a child that would not divide the last sixpence to relieve her. . . ." She did give her son her temper. "Of the mother," a childhood friend of George's recalled, "I was ten times more afraid than of my own parents."[3] Mary Washington influenced her son's choice of a wife: Martha Custis, besides being cute, rich, and a shrewd businesswoman, was calm, devoted, and never gave her husband a moment's trouble.

Washington's early life is too misty to explain the family dynamics. All that stands out is the lack of positively engaging parental figures, especially paternal ones.

Washington never became a parent himself. Martha Custis was twenty-seven years old when he married her in 1759, and she had given birth four times in her first marriage. There is no account of an illegitimate child of Washington's that is more than graffiti on the bathroom wall of history. The conclusion that he was sterile is inescapable. The act of generation, what Seneca called the "least part" of the benefit of life, was one he could not perform.

From time to time he tried to escape the conclusion nevertheless. After he had resigned his commission as Commander in Chief in 1783, he wrote to Congress asking if he could have the paper back, since it might "serve *my grandchildren* some fifty or a hundred years hence for a theme to ruminate upon. . . ."[4] Both he and Martha were over fifty, and they had been married for almost a quarter of a century. If they were going to have any children, they would have had them by then. Still he ruminated.

Six years later, the subject came up again, though in a very different way. In the discarded draft of his first inaugural, in a passage that the historian-vandal managed not to damage beyond repair, Washington was prepared to acknowledge his childlessness publicly. ". . . it will be recollected," he wrote "that the Divine Providence hath not seen fit, that my blood should be transmitted or my name perpetuated by the endearing, though sometimes seducing channel of immediate offspring. I have no child for whom I could wish to make a provision—no family to build in greatness upon my country's ruins." This lack, he argued, made him more fit to be entrusted with the presidency. "Let then the Adversaries to this Constitution . . . point to the sinister object, or to the earthly consideration beyond the hope of rendering some little service to our parent country, that could have persuaded me to accept this appointment." Washington's wistful letter to Congress had been written at the beginning of his sixth decade; as he neared the end of it, he accepted his personal loss, and though he never gave the speech, in his own mind he transmuted the loss into a political benefit.

The dynastic temptation was very real. The country was lucky that there was so little material for temptation to work with. Of the first five presidents, only John Adams had sons who survived to adulthood. Jefferson, Madison, and Monroe, whose administrations covered the first quarter of the nineteenth century, were known as the "Virginia dynasty," but if the seducing channel of immediate (male) offspring had flowed from any of them, the dynasty might have extended into a second generation. How much more likely would this have been the case for literal sons of Washington. None of these men would have tolerated a son becoming president by any means except election. But a gaggle of junior Washingtons, Jeffersons, Madisons, and Monroes could have crowded the political landscape intolerably. As it was, John Adams's eldest son, John Quincy Adams, became the sixth president.

Lacking descendants of his own, Washington turned to three substitutes. The first were his stepchildren and stepgrandchildren. Two of Martha's four children survived infancy: a daughter, Patsy, who was sickly and died at seventeen; and a son, Jack, who married and lived to be twenty-seven. Washington worried about Jack's education, writing one tutor that he wanted him "fit for more useful purposes, than a horse Racer," and he worried about his behavior when Jack was elected to the Virginia State Senate during the war: "I do not suppose that so young a Senator, as you are . . . can yet have much influence in a populous assembly. . . . But it is in your power to be punctual in your attendance. . . ." He expended the same anxious attention on Jack's son, George Washington Parke Custis. But he never considered the Custis brood his own, and they never considered him theirs. ". . . his own near relatives feared to speak or laugh before him," remembered Nelly Custis, one of Jack's daughters, ". . . not from his severity," but out of "awe and respect. . . . When he entered a room where we were all mirth and in high conversation, all were instantly mute. He would sit a short time and then retire, quite provoked and disappointed. . . ."[5]

A second group of surrogate children was his staff during the Revolutionary War, which he called his "family." Several of these men had lost their own fathers early in life. Lafayette's had been killed in battle when he was two. Hamilton's left his children and their mother (whom he had never married) when Hamilton was ten. They met Washington at impressionable ages: Lafayette was nineteen, Hamilton twenty-two. Washington himself was forty-five. His relationship with Lafayette was nearly cloudless. Lafayette's long political career in France would be marred by enthusiasm, bad judgment, and what Jefferson (who liked him) cruelly called a "canine appetite" for popularity, but when he was in America, these vices had the form of ingenuousness. A week after they met, Washington apologized for the unprofessionalism of his army. "It is not to teach but to learn that I come hither," Lafayette replied.[6] They slept on the ground under one blanket after the Battle of Monmouth. Lafayette named his eldest son Georges Washington. Washington's relationship with Hamilton was longer, and hence more complicated. Jefferson, whose father had died when he was fourteen, never served on Washington's staff and had important early mentors besides his political colleague— who was only one decade older, not two. But he too felt the tug of admiration, which envenomed his relations with Hamilton all the more. Saddest of the protégés was Edmund Randolph— taken into Washington's "family" at age twenty-two, after his Tory father left for England; disgraced by his political father twenty years later.

But the most important category of substitute descendants was not the children who grew up in Washington's house or the younger men of his staff or his cabinet (who sometimes acted childishly enough), but the future generations of Americans. The transposition was quite conscious on Washington's part. In the spring of 1783, as peace was coming and the army was winding up its affairs, he twice used a striking phrase. In a letter to a staff officer, he hoped that the "Peace and Independency for which we have fought" would be "a blessing to Millions yet unborn," and in the Circular to the States, he warned that "our fate" was bound up with "the destiny of unborn Millions."[7] This was a more particularized image than "the destiny of the republican form of government," which he would invoke in the first Inaugural Address that he actually delivered—more particularized and more personal, even though the persons were unknown, unknowable. In 1783, as his letter to Congress showed, he still imagined that the unborn millions might include descendants of his own. But even if he had been the most prolific father in the world, most of them would be the posterity of others—strangers to his blood, as well as strangers to him in time. Mentioning them was an act of adoption.

Six years later, Washington received a printed sermon, which had been delivered in 1759 by a minister in Maine. Washington got sermons all the time; when he acknowledged this one, he added that he "appro[ved] of the doctrine inculcated." The sermon commemorated the death of a Maine hero, Sir William Pepperrell, who fought in two colonial wars and was made a baronet and a general. The text was from Psalm 82, a short psalm addressed to "the mighty" of the earth, which ends by reminding them that "ye shall die like men." What, when the mighty die, should they have accomplished? The minister turned for an answer to a funeral oration quoted by Socrates. "Hereditary Honor is indeed a noble and splendid Patrimony. But to enjoy a fair Estate, either in Fame or Money, and for want of a proper Supply of Wealth and Glory of your own, not to be able to transmit it to your Posterity, is infamous and unmanly."[8] The mighty—the Pepperrells and the Washingtons— should pass on as much honor and riches as they had inherited; here is an echo of the concept of reputation as a precious cargo. But to whom should they pass it? "Hereditary," "Patrimony," and "Posterity" are terms of blood, of literal fathers and children, of those connected by the benefit of life. General Pepperrell had a son; this part of the sermon had been addressed to him. General Washington had no sons. But he could ensure that his "Honor," the reflection of his life lived well, might be a benefit to the millions unborn, his adopted political heirs. This was a doctrine he could approve of.

It is a guess forced on us by a meager record, but a reasonable guess nonetheless, that Washington had partly to construct his own father—to draw the necessary influences out of other men or out of himself. It is undeniable that he had to invent substitute children. The children he settled on were his countrymen.

PATRIARCHS AND MASTERS

Political philosophers have compared government to the family for millennia, but the world shows almost as many different family structures as regimes. Which should a founder adopt? What kind of political father would Washington be? In the fall of 1778, Thomas Paine, the American propagandist, addressed a pamphlet to Britain, the "*Parent country*." ". . . had you studied only the domestic politics of a family," Paine chided, "you would have learned how to govern the state," and would have let the colonies go without a struggle.[1] But suppose the British thought that, in not letting America go, they were doing what parents, and parent countries, were entitled to do? The father of his country faced the same question.

Washington's world offered him a number of competing models of political fatherhood. Not a great number, for he was not a philosopher working in a vacuum nor an anthropologist working from a textbook, but enough so that he had a range of options. Two of them—the Patriot King and the patriarch—

came glancingly into his life. A third—the master—was a model he struggled with for twenty years and vanquished only at the end of his life.

The Patriot King was a hand-me-down slogan of British politics of a generation earlier. Americans took a great interest in British rhetoric of the 1720s and 1730s, particularly the rhetoric of those who had been excluded from the political establishment, for their arguments seemed to apply to the imperial establishment forty years later. The gaudiest of the outsiders was Henry St. John, Viscount Bolingbroke.[2]

As a young man, Bolingbroke once "ran naked through the park in a state of intoxication." As an adult, he impressed even his enemies with his charm and eloquence, and he impresses intellectual historians of the Revolution to this day. He failed as a politician, by attaching himself to a string of sovereigns and would-be sovereigns who all let him down, usually by dying before his schemes could come to fruition. But he had a great success as a journalist, assailing the politicians who had beaten him out of office. His comrades in verbal warfare included Swift and Pope; during his lifetime he was considered their peer.

Bolingbroke's contribution to the politics of fatherhood was the idea of the Patriot King. He first sketched it in a journal named *The Craftsman*. "A *good King* . . . is only another Word for a *royal Patriot*. . . . Though He is the *Father of his People*, He is but the *Son of his Country*, which hath adopted Him into that high Trust; and He owes her a Duty, as well as the meanest of his Subjects; nay, much more is required at his Hands . . . because much more is put into his Power." What was required at his hands was to act as a check on corrupt ministries. Corruption, as Hamilton would observe to Jefferson, was a fixture of British political life and would have characterized a ministry run by Bolingbroke, as much as the ministries of his foes. Nevertheless, Bolingbroke imagined a king determined to root it out: when "the Cries of the People become loud and importunate . . . [t]hey reach the Prince's Ears, and pierce his Heart. He makes Enquiry into their Complaints; and finding them just, rouzes Himself up to Vengeance, and resolves to redress them."[3]

Some years later, Bolingbroke produced a small book on the subject *The Idea of a Patriot King,* which presented the righteous royal father as an ongoing leader of government, rather than an emergency ombudsman. Now the Patriot King's virtue was not only that he was incorruptible. but that he was nonpartisan. He could "govern like the common father of his people" because he was "not exposed to the temptation, of governing by a party." The "true image" of his rule was "that of a patriarchal family, where the head and all the members are united by one common interest, and animated by one common spirit. . . . Instead of abetting the divisions of his people, he will endeavor to unite them . . . instead of putting himself at the head of one party in order to govern his people, he will put himself at the head of his people in order to govern, or more properly to subdue, all parties."[4]

Washington owned a complete set of *The Craftsman*; Adams and Jefferson admired Bolingbroke. From him flow two opposing tendencies in American political thinking: checks and balances as a way of curbing factions, and the fantasy of politics without factions at all. The first got written into the Constitution, but the second has flickered in the American mind like a marshfire, down to Ross Perot. In the 1760s, Americans attached their fantasies of an impartial Patriot King to George III, whom they hoped would curb the imperial busybodies who were beginning to harass them. "May the British Empire be always happy in a patriot King of the House of Brunswick," went one toast offered by prerebellious Bostonians.[5] When

George III disappointed them, they transferred their dreams to Washington—a switch assisted by the fact that the two men had the same first name and profiles similar enough that coin collectors are unable to say whether the nameless big-nosed heads on the faces of crude colonial tokens commemorate the king or the general.

There were problems with the Patriot King as a model for Washington. The most obvious was that the new country had not become a kingdom. Bolingbroke did not imagine that there could be patriot dynasties: the most his hero could do would be to uphold good government during the "whole course of his reign."[6] But republics could have king-equivalents in the form of presidents-for-life: an institution which Hamilton quixotically recommmended at the Constitutional Convention, and which Washington could have enjoyed in fact, if not in form, by staying in office until he died. If one took the Patriot King literally, Bolingbroke was offering the same advice as Colonel Nicola.

The worst thing about the idea of a Patriot King is that it is content-free. The Patriot King will not buy elections (he won't need to, because he inherits the job), and he won't rely on parties (for the same reason), but beyond that, he has no policies and no politics. There are moments when a leader must stand above certain battles: the struggle between Anglo- and Francophiles, so early in the United States's life, was one. But as a formula for long-term government, embodied in an executive, it is nonsense.

The reason the idea is nonsense is that the man who framed it was a scoundrel. (So were most of the politicians of his day, but they did not set up as theorists.) Bolingbroke's ideas have the flimsiness of scaffolding, thrown up to serve some other purpose—in his case, attaining office. He spoke the language of principle, without having any. He doffed allies and dynasties like perukes, writing whatever might undermine those who wielded the powers that he himself coveted. He was less than a journalist; he was the spin doctor for his own lifelong campaign for a job. His rationalizations dazzled his contemporaries in England and America. Fortunately for us, his American admirers had other figures and arguments to act as ballast: intellectual checks and balances.

The politician of the late eighteenth century who took him most seriously was George III. Bolingbroke was a friend of George's father; *The Patriot King* was a text used by the Earl of Bute, George's tutor and later his prime minister. It was not much help to the monarch. Until madness closed in, George III managed British politics with considerable skill, though by the precise means—corruption and faction—that Bolingbroke had professed to deplore. He was less successful with the thirteen colonies.

Another possible model for political fathers was the patriarch. The patriarchs of the Bible were the forefathers of Israel and its twelve tribes, and the eighteenth century (like ours) used the word as a metaphor. Bolingbroke mentioned "the patriarchal spirit" in passing, and Washington's contemporaries often bestowed the title on him, in an equally casual way: when Lafayette sent him the key of the Bastille, he called him liberty's "patriarch." But the word—whether applied to fathers or rulers—could be very precise indeed.

Patriarchy's main defender in the English-speaking world, Sir Robert Filmer, never ran naked through a park and never dazzled anyone. He was a country gentleman of the early seventeenth century, who wrote a number of pamphlets on usury, witches, the Holy Ghost, and other topics, and who took a modest pride in his work: "A dwarf sometimes may see that which a giant looks over." In 1632, he asked the king's secretary whether he might publish a "Discourse . . . in praise of Royaltie." Permission was denied. Almost fifty years later (and nearly thirty years after Filmer's death), his discourse, *Patriarcha*, was published and attacked by horrified liberals, including John Locke.[7]

Filmer's model for fathers was "the lordship which Adam by creation had over the whole world, and [which] by right descending from him the patriarchs did enjoy. . . ." Filmer thought the power of primitive fathers over their families was absolute, and he sifted the Bible for instances, even if they reflected badly on patriarchal judgment: he noted that in the thirty-eighth chapter of Genesis, Judah condemned his daughter-in-law Tamar to death "for playing the harlot," even though he repealed the verdict when he realized that he himself had unwittingly been the man she had played the harlot with.[8]

The first country was the family of Adam. ". . . I see no reason but that we may call Adam's family a commonwealth, except we will wrangle about words. For Adam, living nine hundred and thirty years and seeing seven or eight descents from himself, he might live to command of his children and their posterity a multitude far bigger than many commonwealths or kingdoms." Every subsequent country should be ruled by fatherly command. "There is, and always shall be continued to the end of the world, a natural right of a supreme father over every multitude. . . ." Filmer was not an advocate of tyranny, of the patriarch-father exercising every power he possessed, simply because he possessed it. But he wanted to show that rights were "privileges" derived from "the grace and bounty of princes," not from natural law, and that there could be no question of the multitude sharing in the right to rule.[9] Here was an answer, decades ahead of time, to Paine's breezy confidence that he knew how parents and parent countries ought to behave. Filmer made his own study of the politics of the family and came up with very different principles for governing the state.

Patriarchs and Masters

However crude his arguments or incredible his theology, Filmer deserves to be considered a serious man—unlike Bolingbroke. Men must live, one way or another, and if they cannot live by ruling themselves, they will submit to the rule of others. Filmer tried to explain and justify a common human situation.

The great challenge to Washington in patriarchy was Filmer's bland combination of liberty and power—his acknowledgment that men enjoyed freedoms, and his insistence that they were princely gifts. The congressman who cried when Washington spoke, the women who found him charming, the soldiers who thought him superb, stood in danger of making the same mistake, as much as the African poetess and the Irish colonel who wished him a throne. The challenge was greater because there were moments when Washington had to direct men as surely as a rider directs a horse. So he always had to find a way of directing them back to an understanding of their rights.

Filmer's principles had a strange afterlife on another continent, in another century. A number of Filmer's peers and neighbors were involved in founding the Virginia Company in 1606. Filmer's younger brother, Edward, moved to Virginia; so did one of his sons, whose widow, Mary Filmer, became related by a second marriage to most of the founding families of the colony. These transplanted Englishmen were not self-conscious Filmerites; despite his posthumous revival, Filmer never had a reputation like Bolingbroke's. But they shared Filmer's frame of mind. Royalist country gentlemen of the seventeenth and eighteenth centuries honored the king, but wanted government to leave them alone, to run their neighborhoods and their families as they saw fit. They were patriarchs of the private sector. When they crossed the Atlantic—and many of the Virginia gentry (including the Washingtons) were descendants of Royalist country families—they took this mindset with them. "Like one of the patriarchs," said William Byrd II, "I have my flocks and my herds, my bond-men and bond-women, and every sort of trade amongst my own servants, so that I live in a kind of independence [from] every one, but Providence."[10] When George III threatened this independence, the latter-day patriarchs of Virginia turned against him. But the patriarchal disposition, if unmodified, would have sanctioned rebellion for the sake of custom merely.

There were customary rebels on the American side. In the fall of 1776, after writing the Declaration of Independence, Jefferson returned to Virginia where he proposed restrictions on entail—the power to control inheritance in land over more than one generation (a power patriarchs who did not live as long as Adam had to rely on, if they wanted to impose their lordship for nine hundred and thirty years). One Virginia planter wrote a choleric letter to General Washington, who presumably had other things on his mind, denouncing Jefferson's proposal as an assault on the "right to do as we please with our own property," which he said was the "basis of the American contest." He also called Jefferson a "drunkard," thus showing that eccentric squires did not exist only in England, or in comic novels.[11] In the end, entail was abolished altogether.

Filmer himself had already made a second posthumous comeback. On the eve of the Revolution, the Reverend Jonathan Boucher, an Anglican minister in Prince Georges County, Maryland, preached a sermon on politics that, as historian Peter Laslett put it, was "pure Filmerism." "It was not to be expected from an all-wise and all-merciful Creator," the minister said, "that, having formed creatures capable of order and rule, he should turn them loose into the world . . . that, like so many wild beasts, they might tear and worry one another. . . ." So, "[a]s soon as there were some to be governed, there were also some to govern. . . . The first father was the first king . . . it was thus that all government originated; and monarchy is it's most ancient form." Boucher was no obscure parson; he had tutored the children of many Virginia notables, most notably Jack Custis. Twenty-two years later, when Boucher published his American sermons in England, he dedicated them to Jack's stepfather, "George Washington Esquire . . . I was once your neighbor and your friend."[12] So the follower of one long-dead country gentleman greeted the Virginia gentleman who had so unaccountably turned revolutionary.

Boucher spoke, not only for the losing side, but for an arcane faction of it. He acknowledged, in a footnote to his published sermon, that Filmer was by then known chiefly as Locke's butt. In the decade after independence, many of the features of small-scale patriarchy—primogeniture, as well as entail—were altered or abolished. The one feature of patriarchy that remained, and put down ever deeper roots, was slavery, and it offered Washington a third model of political fatherhood.

"How is it," asked Dr. Johnson in 1775, "that we hear the loudest *yelps* for liberty among the drivers of Negroes?" He was not the last person to ask. "Oh! happy Carolina! happy, thrice Virginia!" wrote a Federalist journalist during Washington's second term. "After having spent the day in singing hymns to the Goddess of Liberty, the virtuous Democrat gets him home to his peaceful dwelling, and sleeps, with his *property* secure beneath his roof, yea, sometimes in his very *arms*. . . ."[13] The contrast between ideals and practice has amused the Revolution's enemies and embarrassed many of its friends for two hundred years. We are not finished yet, either with the broad issue or with the sexual taunt, as the continuing popularity of the story of Jefferson's supposed affair with Sally Hemings attests.

Founding Father

Americans were not the only patrons of the institution of slavery at the time of independence. They bought their slaves from African dealers. Though the Chief Justice of the King's Bench had ruled in 1772 that any slave who set foot in Britain became free, slavery was not touched in the colonies, where nearly all of the slaves in the empire lived. Slavery was sanctioned by the Bible and by Aristotle. But, alone in a world of slaveholders, Americans brought on themselves the charge of hypocrisy, because of their principles and their rhetoric. They not only declared that all men were created equal, they characterized the imperial legislation that was passed in London, and the measures taken to enforce it, as acts of enslavement, to which they would not submit. Washington used the rhetoric of resistance to slavery regularly. The British ministry, he wrote George William Fairfax in June 1774, "are endeavoring . . . to fix the Shackles of Slavery upon us." They would not succeed, he wrote Bryan Fairfax a month later, "till they have first reduced us to the most abject state of slavery that ever was designed for mankind." "The crisis is come when we must assert our rights," he wrote Bryan again, cutting even closer to the bone, or become "as tame and abject slaves, as the blacks we rule over with such arbitrary sway." Once the fighting began, the British offered freedom to any slave who would run away from a rebel owner. When the last colonial Governor of Virginia started an abortive counterrevolution in the state, Washington wrote from Boston that he was "an arch-traitor to the rights of humanity . . . if he gets formidable, numbers [of negroes] will be tempted to join" him. Seventeen of Washington's slaves joined the arch-traitors in 1781, when a British sloop sailed up the Potomac and bombarded Mount Vernon. Washington recovered two of them six months later when the British surrendered at Yorktown. The British liberation was not a philanthropic project: they sent slaves who had smallpox back to rebel plantations, as a form of human germ warfare, and during the siege of Yorktown, one American soldier noted "herds of Negroes" that the British had "turned adrift . . . with pieces of ears of burnt Indian corn in the hands and mouths, even of those that were dead."[14] But the British were not fighting a war in the name of inalienable rights.

We wonder how Washington encompassed the contradictions. One way he did was the way that all men, including ourselves, encompass their contradictions: by not thinking about them. During the war, Hamilton and John Laurens, another young officer on his staff, proposed to raise a black regiment in South Carolina, Laurens' home state, and "give them their freedom with their swords." Washington raised a few objections: the army lacked weapons; slaves who remained in bondage would be discontent. "But," he concluded, "as this is a subject that has never employed much of my thoughts, these are no more than the first crude Ideas that have struck me. . . ."[15]

But the subject did employ his thoughts at other times, and they can be followed in his words and actions. As a matter of public policy, Washington hoped that slavery might end, though he had no plan for ending it—which meant, in practice, that he acquiesced in the status quo. In the spring of 1786, he wrote a letter to Robert Morris in Philadelphia which made one of his bluntest statements against slavery. ". . . [T]here is not a man living who wishes more sincerely than I do, to see a plan adopted for the abolition of it. . . . there is only one proper and effectual mode by which it can be accomplished, and that is by Legislative authority; and this, as far as my suffrage will go, shall never be wanting." But Washington was writing Morris in the first place in behalf of a fellow Virginian who had become the target of a "vexatious lawsuit" brought by Philadelphia Quakers, for the purpose of liberating a slave he had taken to the city. Washington told Morris that such *ad hoc* actions bred "discontent" in slaves and "resentment" in slave-holders.[16] His asperity on the subject of Quaker abolitionists may also have owed something to his recollection of Quakers refusing to bear arms during the grim campaigning in New Jersey and Pennsylvania ten years earlier; how was it that he heard the loudest yelps for liberty from those unwilling to fight for it?

A month after his letter to Morris, he was writing Lafayette, congratulating him on a scheme to buy a plantation in French Guiana and populate it with liberated slaves. The *but*s in Washington's letter mark the stasis in which he found himself. "Would to God a like spirit would diffuse itself generally into the minds of the people of this country; *but* I despair of seeing it. Some petitions were presented to the Assembly, at its last Session, for the abolition of slavery, *but* they could scarcely obtain a reading. To set [slaves] afloat at once would, I really believe, be productive of much inconvenience and mischief; *but* by degrees it certainly might, and assuredly ought to be effected; and that too by legislative authority [emphasis added]."[17] But how was this to be done, if no one would propose a way to do it?

Nothing during his presidency forced him to confront the issue. Policies that were in effect pro- or antislavery were dictated by other considerations—he helped France suppress a slave revolt in Santo Domingo and refused to pressure Britain to return escaped American slaves to their former owners, because he did not want to provoke either country—while the disputes that would tear America apart in the next century, over the status of slavery in new states and in territories, did not arise. Politically, nothing drove him from his place, and he stayed in it.

His conduct as a slave-owning president was guided by reticence. He brought slaves from Mount Vernon to serve him in New York and Philadelphia. He kept them out of visible positions, and when he left office, he freed some of them by discreetly leaving them behind (so discreetly that the deed was only discovered by his biographer James Thomas Flexner sifting his correspondence a hundred and seventy years later). He made an attempt to recover a runaway during his second term, when Oney Judge, one of Martha's young women, appeared to have eloped to New Hampshire with a Frenchman. Fearing that she had been seduced and fearing the example of a successful escape, Washington asked the collector of customs in Portsmouth to send her back, if it could be done without "excit[ing] . . . a riot." When the collector replied that it could not, Washington let the matter drop. In both cases of the slaves who got their freedom, the President was sensitive to public opinion. He left his slaves in Philadelphia on the sly, because southern Republicans, who were already disaffected with his administration, would have howled if he had done it publicly, and he left Oney Judge in New Hampshire lest he provoke "uneasy sensations" among northerners.[18]

In his private life, as a slaveowner, he maintained a plantation that was as good as such things went. A Polish visitor in the 1790s thought that Washington treated his slaves "more humanely" than other Virginians treated theirs (the Pole also thought the slave quarters were "more miserable" than the worst cottages of Polish peasants). There has never been a credible tale of Washington taking advantage of a slave sexually; the few incredible tales derive from a wartime forgery, in which British journalists inserted a sentence about "pretty little Kate, the washerwoman's daughter" into the published text of a letter to Washington from another planter. There is an authentic account of a white man *not* having sex with Washington's slaves. "Will you believe it, I have not humped a single mulatto since I am here," an aide to Baron von Steuben complained in a letter from Mount Vernon in 1784.[19] Whether the man's failure was because of his incompetence, the mulattos' unwillingness, or the tenor of life at Mount Vernon is not known.

But being as good as such things went was not good enough. Washington pursued three plans to lessen the evil.

One was a holding operation, though it had major consequences. Beginning in the early 1770s, he rarely bought a slave, and he would not sell one, unless the slave consented, which never happened. Not selling slaves was an economic loss. Slave labor on a plantation with soil as poor as Mount Vernon brought in little or nothing. Washington had abandoned tobacco, because the merchants were exigent and the prices bad, but nothing else he turned to did more than make ends meet. The only profit a man in his position could make was by selling slaves to states where agriculture was more flourishing. Washington would not. "I am principled against selling negroes, as you would do cattle at a market. . . ."[20] From 1775 until his death, the slave population at Mount Vernon more than doubled.

His second plan, conceived in 1793, would have ended his career as a plantation owner. In December he wrote Arthur Young, the English editor of *Annals of Agriculture*, a journal that serious farmers on both sides of the Atlantic read (George III was a contributor). "[F]rom . . . causes which are not necessary to detail," he proposed to break up Mount Vernon into four farms, to be rented to "four substantial farmers," while he retained only the main house. In passing (the letter runs on for many pages) he mentioned that "many of the negroes, male and female, might be hired by the year, as labourers." In a private letter to his secretary, he noted that this was the chief motive for his offer—"to liberate a certain species of property which I possess very repugnantly to my own feelings."[21] The scheme was intricate: no farm could be rented in advance of the others, to avoid discontenting slaves that were not yet freed (the same objection he had raised to the Laurens-Hamilton plan for a black regiment). It was drastic: to abate his repugnance, he was willing to surrender his way of life, except for the symbolic shell of his house. It turned out to be unrealistic, for Washington and Young found no takers.

His last plan was embodied in his will. The second of its fourteen items concerned his slaves, and it was a detailed and emphatic clause. There was no rhetoric in it (there was little in the entire will); it was concerned to get the job done. All of his slaves were to be freed at his wife's death. Old slaves or children without parents should "be comfortably cloathed and fed by my heirs"; the children should be taught to read and write and "be brought up to some useful occupation," until they turned twenty-five. A "regular and permanent fund" should be established for these purposes, instead of "trusting to the uncertain provision" of individuals. No slave should be sold "under any pretext whatsoever"—this was underlining, to thwart kidnappers who sold free blacks into slavery (a crime, to be sure, but not one that was zealously pursued). Then more underlining: "I . . . most pointedly, and most solemnly enjoin it upon my Executors . . . to see that *this* clause respecting Slaves, and every part thereof be religiously fulfilled at the Epoch at which it is directed to take place; without evasion, neglect, or delay. . . ." The tone of command, after years of small silent deeds and private regrets, shows what an uphill path, for himself and his society, Washington was taking, even in a last will and testament. Perhaps it also shows his own pent-up repugnance. Martha Washington released her husband's slaves before she died, in December 1800. The estate supported pensioners until 1833.

During Washington's life, both approval and disapproval of slavery were found among slaveowners and nonslaveowners alike. All four permutations were expressed at the Constitutional Convention. "Religion & humanity had nothing to do with this question. Interest alone is the governing principle with nations" (John Rutledge, South Carolina). "The morality or wisdom of slavery are considerations belonging to the States themselves. What enriches a part enriches the whole" (Oliver Ellsworth, Connecticut). Slavery "bring[s] the judgment of heaven on a Country" (George Mason, Virginia). "It was the curse of heaven on the States where it prevailed" (Gouverneur Morris, Pennsylvania).[22] Washington belonged, with Mason and Jefferson, in the hardest category—disapproving owners. Theirs was the most difficult position to maintain, psychologically and rhetorically. It would not be maintained over the next sixty years, as southern antislavery rhetoric withered. Practically and politically, disapproving owners were in the hardest position from which to achieve their goals. How do you weaken an institution in which you and all your neighbors are enmeshed? Washington did enough, finally, to free his own slaves, which was more than many owners in his position did. Jefferson never freed all his, nor did any of the other slave-owning presidents.

It was not enough to free the country. Slavery proved to be the most tenacious form of patriarchy, and even as the disapproving owners fell silent, the approving owners came to justify what they did on the grounds of religion and humanity, as well as interest. Slavery could be a form of political fatherhood too, with the patriarch benignly presiding over his bondmen and bondwomen, and Robert Filmer himself made a third comeback in the 1860s, to be rummaged for justifications.[23] Resolving the question of slavery was a task for the unborn millions. Washington managed to extricate himself, even if only posthumously, from the role of slaveowner.

FATHER OF HIS COUNTRY

The kind of father Washington sought to be was the father who, when his children become adults, lets them go. That was the difference between him and a Patriot King, a patriarch, or a master. Such political fathers may rule badly or wisely, but they rule for life. Washington stepped aside, not, as Paine believed, because all fathers do, but because he chose to. He was conscious of the momentousness of the choice. The United States should not be left to prove, he wrote Lafayette in 1788, that "Mankind [was] made for a Master."[1] After years of hesitation and denial, he gave up slavery, the last form of mastership in his life.

A political father who steps aside does so because he sees the likeness between himself and his countrymen. It is an incomplete likeness in many ways, for political as for actual fathers. Children know less than their parents, average men are inferior to great men, and citizens cannot have exactly the same duties and powers as rulers, unless there is no government at all, and everyone carves for himself. But the likeness is there, because children grow up, and because great men and rulers are still men. Washington's chosen form of fatherhood complemented his political theory and his manners. The rights of man and the rules of civility urged him to the conclusion that he should be the father of a country whose people would rule their own lives.

The most theatrical and theater-loving of presidents kept quoting Addison, but he could have seen more of himself, and his choice of fatherhood, in Shakespeare. *King Lear*, even with its eighteenth-century happy ending, is a tragedy that is set in motion when a political father steps aside incompletely, without realizing the implications of the act. ". . . 'tis our fast intent/ To shake all cares and business from our age,/ Conferring them on younger strengths," Lear announces in the first scene, and proceeds to divide his kingdom among his daughters. But a few speeches later, he adds a condition: he will keep his royal title and one hundred knights. It doesn't work, because it couldn't. Goneril and Regan, the wicked daughters, did not have to throw him out into a storm, but even if they had been Cordelias, he could not have continued to keep power over them after giving it up.

The Tempest, which Washington saw in Dryden's version and to which he alluded in letters, is the dream version of a father and a ruler stepping aside; perhaps because it is a dream, it goes better. Prospero, the duke/magician driven into exile before the play begins, rules with his charms his daughter, the rebellious subjects who have fallen into his hands, a spirit, and a slave; the problems of politics, and family politics, are transmuted into symbols and managed by magic. But in the last act, Prospero releases everyone, with full consciousness of what he is doing. His daughter will marry, Ariel will vanish, Caliban and his enemies, all chastened, will be pardoned. "My charms I'll break, their senses I'll restore,/ And they shall be themselves." Washington dealt with men in all their gnarled reality, not archetypes. Even so, he found the way to let go successfully.

Living after Washington, and under the principles he upheld, we think of letting go as the easy choice, yet it could not have been. Retirement is a foretaste of mortality. ("Now he terrifies me," Rilke would write of Prospero: "The way he draws/ the wire into his head, and hangs himself/ beside the other puppets. . . .")[2] It is no accident that *resignation* means leaving office and accepting fate. How difficult resignation must have been for a man who loved uniforms, activity, and office as much as he loved his vine and fig tree—for though he always came back to Mount Vernon, he always left it, when the call came. How much more difficult it must have been when, in order to work out the moral proposition to which he had committed himself, he proposed to let most of Mount Vernon go.

But Washington was not the only one for whom letting go was difficult; it was difficult for his contemporaries and for the unborn millions. When a political father lets go, then his political children are on their own, with all the uncertainty that entails. Washington foresaw their situation in the third paragraph of his first Farewell Address, the Circular to the States. In a lifetime of solid paragraphs, buttressed with precise, sometimes intricate, clauses, this is the most carefully wrought, as well as the most startling. It is worth quoting in full, because it is about us.

The paragraph consists of only three sentences, the first two of them enormously long. It opens with a panoramic establishing shot.

"The Citizens of America, placed in the most enviable conditions, as the sole Lords and Proprietors of a vast Tract of Continet, comprehending all the various soils and climates of the World, and abounding with all the necessaries and conveniencies of life, are now by the late satisfactory pacification, acknowledged to be possessed of absolute freedom and Independency; They are, from this period, to be considered as the Actors [the favorite metaphor] on a most conspicuous Theatre, which seems to be peculiarly designated by Providence for the display of human greatness and felicity; Here, they are not only surrounded with every thing which can contribute to the completion of private and domestic enjoyment, but Heaven has crowned all its other blessings, by giving a fairer oppertunity for political happiness, than any other Nation has ever been favored with."

Washington has set a scene of thousands of miles and metaphysical importance, for he has established North America as the stage and Providence as the producer. But he also, at the end, introduces a human concept, "political happiness," which is the business of the next sentence.

"Nothing can illustrate these observations more forcibly, than a recollection of the happy conjuncture of times and circumstances, under which our Republic assumed its rank among the Nations; The foundation of our empire was not laid in the gloomy age of Ignorance and Superstition, but at an Epocha when the rights of mankind were better understood and more clearly defined, than at any former period; the researches of the human mind, after social happiness, have been carried to a great extent; the Treasures of knowledge, acquired through a long succession of years, by the labours of Philosophers, Sages and Legislatures, are laid open for our use, and their collected wisdom may be happily applied in the Establishment of our forms of Government; the free cultivation of Letters, the unbounded extension of Commerce, the progressive refinement of Manners, the growing liberality of sentiment, and above all, the pure and benign light of Revelation, have had a meliorating influence on mankind and increased the blessings of Society."

He is like a lawyer, enumerating bequests, or a team of long-shoremen, tirelessly loading a ship. He began by giving us a continent and invoking Providence; here he credits to our account the rights of man, abstract and practical knowledge, the arts, trade, good behavior, and Christianity (so long as it is not superstitious). Now for the climax:

"At this auspicious period, the United States came into existence as a Nation, and if their Citizens should not be completely free and happy, the fault will be intirely their own."[3]

The shock of this sentence is partly stylistic. After its long compound predecessors, as relentless as breakers on a beach, it seems terse, almost curt. The real shock is the thought. After such a stem-winding warm-up, we expect an affirmation; a keynote speech to end all keynotes; Fourth of July rhetoric seven years after the first Fourth of July, when it was still fresh. Instead, we get a warning so blunt that it is almost a rebuke. With so many blessings, how could we fail? Easily enough, he tells us; see that you don't.

It is one of the most sobering moments in any major American speech—even more sobering than the bleak mysticism of Lincoln's Second Inaugural. Washington is saying that America's political success is problematic. In saying so, he fingers a paradox in the doctrine of natural rights. If you believe in the rights of man, you believe that they are grounded in nature—that they are, as Jefferson put it, "inalienable." But that does not necessarily mean—and Washington did not believe—that establishing a government based on those rights is easy, or even possible. This is why, in his First Inaugural Address, six years later, he spoke of the "Republican model of government" in its American form as an "experiment." It was as much of an experiment as Franklin's key and his kite; more so, since Franklin was pretty sure beforehand that the key would glow. Washington was not sure that the United States would work. What were the precedents? The Greek example, as Hamilton said, was "disgust[ing]." The Roman Republic had fallen. There were a few republics in recent European history, none of them large. The United Netherlands collapsed in 1787; France would have a revolution in 1789, Santo Domingo (or Haiti) in 1791— hardly encouraging examples. Like Unitarians in theology, Washington as a political philosopher believed in at most one right form of government.

Washington was also saying that responsibility for the experiment's success was only partly his. He would do what he could. When he distributed the Circular to the States, he believed that his task as a founder and father was done. It turned out to be less than half done. But even when it was finished, it was only all that he could do. The rest was up to the "Citizens of America"; is up to us. When he passed through Trenton on his way to his first inauguration, the hopeful banner over the bridge at Assunpink Creek said that the defender of the mothers would be the protector of the daughters. He cannot protect the daughters of the daughters.

This may be the deepest source of our distance from him— the resentment and puzzlement that come from being let go. He seems cryptic, like an oracle that has fallen silent. We feel bereaved. He fought for self-government; we govern ourselves; what now?

Henry Adams (John's great-grandson) captured this sense of abandonment in a recollection of his first visit to Mount Vernon, which he had made in 1850, when he was twelve years old. The mansion was a pilgrimage site, and a move to restore it had begun. So had the final struggle between slave states and free states. The road young Adams took from Washington, D.C., to Mount Vernon was bad. "To the New England mind . . . [b]ad roads meant bad morals. The moral of this Virginia road was clear. . . . Slavery was wicked, and slavery was the cause of this road's badness which amounted to social crime—and yet, at the end of the road and product of the crime stood Mount Vernon and George Washington." Adams is having fun with the certainties and the perplexities of his preadolescent self. But the perplexities were real, and later he strikes a more anxious note. Washington was "like the Pole Star. . . . Mount Vernon always remained where it was, with no practicable road to reach it." Adams put his memory of the unreachable Washington in the context of the debate over slavery, where Washington's accomplishment was entirely private and the least useful publicly. But the feeling of loss and withdrawal clings to the entire career of a political father like Washington. He committed few blunders, and no crimes. He performed every task that came to him, even retirement. His character, as Jefferson put it in his final, measured judgment, "was, in its mass, perfect, in nothing bad, in few points indifferent."[4] Is that all? What good does that do us when we are grown, and he is gone?

It is easier to deal with the legacies of heroes whose careers have been cut short. Murder was a great boost to the reputations of Martin Luther King, Jr., and Abraham Lincoln. Even the death of sixty-two-year-old Franklin Roosevelt seemed untimely, because it occurred in office. Sudden death leaves room for fantasy. *What if Lincoln had presided over Reconstruction? Would Roosevelt have fought the Cold War?* Martyrs become our companions; they keep us in thrall. When a hero concludes his career and Nature concludes his life, we feel excluded.

One way we try to keep in touch with the famous dead is through their words. If their words ring in our ears, we can talk with them in our imaginations. This is why the eloquent fare so well in American history: Lincoln foremost, with Jefferson a close second; Hamilton, Madison, and perhaps Franklin leading the pack. It will be interesting to see what survives of the fireside chats when the last Americans who heard them have died. Occasionally, a mute is boosted by the words of others: if Eisenhower is thought better of now than he was when he left office, that is because he was memorably reassessed by Murray Kempton. But words are shifty, especially the words of the dead; their books can be as deceitful as ouija boards. Even public utterances as straightforward as the Declaration of Independence or the Gettysburg Address can be tugged into the most fantastic shapes. When a great man is articulate *and* protean, like Jefferson, writing one thing one day and something slightly, or very, different the next, then the collected works are ransacked for bumper stickers, and real confusion ensues.

Washington does not belong to the lively, but untrustworthy category of the speaking dead. He never said the most famous words he ever said. "I cannot tell a lie" was put in his mouth by Parson Weems; "entangling alliances" expresses one of his thoughts, but the phrase is from Jefferson's first inaugural (the Farewell Address warned against "permanent Alliances"). Washington's battlefield utterances are blurred by the memories of old men. We know he said something harsh to Charles Lee, but we will never know exactly what. His writings are impressive, but they were reactive, and the effect they make is cumulative. He wrote to respond to demands and to get things done; his patterns of expression and thought reveal themselves slowly. Appreciating Washington's spoken and written words takes time and effort—as much time and effort as it takes to decode his deeds.

There is one last service that the political father can perform, even after letting go. That is to be taken into the country's mind—internalized as an object, as psychoanalysts put it. Americans, as worshippers of youth and newness, are uncomfortable with the notion. When we see the process in others or in ourselves—"He looks just like his dad;" "I know what my mother must have felt"—we note it with amusement or a vague regret. Norman Bates at the end of *Psycho* is the horror version. But internalizing is something everyone must do to grow up. Living as a man or a woman depends on images that we carry with us. Most people internalize their parents as objects, for good or for ill, supplementing them with aspects of important mentors. These images are different from fantasy figures—the Kings or the Lincolns who never got the chance to fix everything for us. They are models, based on the actual behavior of others, shaping the actual behavior of ourselves.

A political father can serve as a model for a nation as a whole—for its citizens individually, or for all of them acting together. It is not a matter of discovering what the hero thought two hundred years ago about a particular issue, or even imagining what he might think about an issue today; it is more a matter of thinking *how* he would think, and judge, and proceed. None of us is going to found a country. But many of us are fathers or fulfill other parental roles. Each of us is the parent of his life. Do we know that the first form of self-government is governing ourselves—not through indifference or rigidity, but through respecting our fellows and wanting to play an honorable part in the world? Do we derive our notions of respect and our definitions of honor from our ideas of right and wrong? Do we have the strength and the heart to make them real? We are all citizens: we pay taxes, and if we're not felons we vote. How well is the experiment of our country going? Do we love our rights so much that we would resent laws we had no role in making as slavery? Do we love others enough that if we had unwarranted power over their lives, we would struggle to give it up? Do we teach our principles and honor those who upheld them? Do we understand that liberty isn't a vacation from restraint, but a duty to govern? That is the model that Washington's life gives us; that is his patrimony.

But the father of his country cannot be a model without

Founding Father

help. The help he needs is memory. "Had he lived in the days of idolatry," wrote an American of Washington in 1777, "he had been worshipped as a god."[5] He didn't live then, he lived here. We can go to his house; we can stand in the room where the Constitution was debated; we can see the places where his soldiers drowned and died and prevailed. If we see them with understanding and sympathy, we can glimpse him.

DEATH

Washington signed his will on July 9, 1799. In it, he apologized for having drawn it up himself: if it "appear[ed] crude and incorrect," that was because "no professional character has been consulted, or has had any Agency in the draught. . . ." It was a private document, apportioning property and mementos to relatives and friends, with a surveyor's particularity: "All the land North of the Road leading from the ford of Dogue run to the Gum spring . . . until it comes to the Stone and three red or Spanish Oaks on the knowl." But some public points appeared nonetheless.

He made his last argument for a national university, leaving his stock in the Potomac Company to set one up. Though two of the signers of the Constitution had gone to college in Britain, and Colonel Laurens had been educated in Geneva, without evident harm, Washington wanted Americans to stay home. Those who went abroad ran the risk of contracting "principles unfriendly to Republican Governmt.," as well as "habits of dissipation and extravagence." Perhaps the two were related. But Washington was as suspicious of William and Mary and Harvard as he was of Oxford and Cambridge. Only in a national university would students "free themselves" from "local prejudices and habitual jealousies." His will was no more effectual in bringing this about than his proposals to Congress had been. His stock in the James River Company did go to a school that became Washington and Lee, a worthy but intensely local college.

He left his swords to his five nephews, with an injunction "not to unsheath them for the purpose of shedding blood, except it be for self defence, or in defence of their Country and its rights; and in the latter case, to keep them unsheathed, and prefer falling with them in their hands, to the relinquishment thereof." This is the only part of the will that verges on rhetoric. It is justified by the fact that swords had not just been props for him.

He disposed of one gift he had been given, a potentially disruptive one, like the apple Paris had awarded Aphrodite. David Erskine, Earl of Buchan, was a liberal nobleman and a founder of the Scottish Society of Antiquaries. He had sent Washington a box made from the tree under which another national hero, Sir William Wallace, had taken refuge after a battle, asking him "to pass it, on the event of my decease, to the man in my country, who should appear to merit it best. . . ." Washington returned it with thanks to the Earl. The country was his political legatee, and he would not entail even something as insubstantial as a trophy to an individual.

The will began and ended with two quiet boasts. "I George Washington of Mount Vernon, a citizen of the United States and lately President of the same. . . . In witness of all, and of each of the things herein contained, I have set my hand and Seal, this ninth day of July, in the year One thousand seven hundred and ninety and of the Independence of the United States the twenty fourth." His pen slipped on the year A.D., but he made no mistake about the age of the United States.

He kept an interest in politics, urging John Marshall, a veteran and a successful lawyer, to run for Congress as a Federalist; he wrote anxious letters to Federalist hard-liners about the possibility of war with France and the rascality (as he now saw it) of the Republicans. But he rebuffed all talk of seeking a third term. A letter to Governor Trumbull, a month after he signed his will, made the point bluntly, and incidentally offered a theory of politics. Trumbull had written that a Washington candidacy could unite a divided party. "Here then, my dear Sir," Washington answered, "let me ask, what satisfaction, what consolation, what safety, should I find in support, which depends on caprice? If *Men*, not *Principles*, can influence . . . the Federalists, what but fluctuations are to be expected?" Washington seems to be arguing the case for principles too strictly. Although theorists and verbalists often talk as if principles were historically autonomous, they depend on men to make their way in the world, as Washington, of all men, should have known. Yet he was right to insist on principles after all, for if the indispensable men are not guided by them, they succumb to improvisation and drift, and ultimately, perhaps, worse. "If [the Federalists] do divide on so *important* a point, it would be dangerous to trust them on any other; and none except those who might be solicitous to fill the Chair of Government would do it."[1] That last clause was prophetic; a year and a half later, the desperate Federalists, throwing principles to the winds, would scheme with Aaron Burr to keep Jefferson out of the White House. They were never trusted with the national government again.

Washington died at the end of the year. At sixty-seven, he was old for his family: he had lived eighteen years longer than his father; he had outlived all his stepchildren and all his siblings. In 1790, Benjamin Franklin had left him a gold-headed crabtree walking stick, saying that "If it were a sceptre, he has merited it and would become it."[2] In his will, Washington bequeathed the cane to his last surviving brother, Charles. But Charles Washington died in September. On December 12, George went riding in a storm. That night, he came down with an acute sore throat.

There are deaths appropriate to wits, and to saints. "What? The flames already?" quipped Voltaire, when a lampshade by his deathbed caught fire. "Brother Fire, God made you beautiful and strong and useful; I pray you be courteous with me," said St. Francis of Assisi to the coals that had been prescribed to cauterize his failing eyes. There is a death of heroes. In 1759, General James Wolfe, twenty-two years old, lay on the field of his last battle, wounded in three places. When he heard someone shout, "They run," he asked who was running, and when told it was the enemy, he said, "God be praised, I will die in peace." There is a death appropriate to tyrants, and sometimes tyrants die it. We read with a sense of fitness of Hitler and his mistress shooting themselves and burning on a tawdry, pseudo-Wagnerian pyre; of Stalin, making convulsive motions with his arm, as if to fend off wolves.

Washington died the death of civility. During the two days he lingered, he was bled and purged and blistered. His secretary, Tobias Lear, tried to make him comfortable, about as effectually as his doctors tried to make him well. Washington tried to relieve the frustration and fear of his attendants. Before the doctors arrived, he asked one of his overseers to bleed him, but the man blanched. "Don't be afraid," Washington told him. When he took to his bed and Lear rolled him over to help his breathing, he apologized for giving trouble and added, "Well, it is a debt we must pay to each other, and I hope when you want aid of this kind you will find it." On his last night, he assured his doctors that he had known "from my first attack that I should not survive," and later: "I thank you for your attentions, but I pray you to take no more trouble about me."[3] (Rule #44: "When a man does all he can, though it succeed not well, blame not him that did it. . . .") Several times he motioned for Christopher, the servant who stood by the bed, to sit. But Christopher, who had been at his post since morning, remained on his feet. It was as if master and slave were engaged in a contest of civilities, which the slave was determined not to lose.

He died toward midnight on the 14th. Four days later he was buried, without any funeral oration as he had requested. The orations came elsewhere. In honoring his reputation, the Senate understood it the way he himself had—a precious cargo, steered through the trials of public life. "The scene is closed—and we are no longer anxious lest misfortune should sully his glory; he has traveled on to the end of his journey, and carried with him an increasing weight of honor: he has deposited it safely where misfortune can not tarnish it; where malice can not blast it." But Representative Marshall spoke more truly: "Our WASHINGTON is no more! the hero . . . lives now only in his own great actions, and in the hearts of an affectionate and afflicted people."[4] The actions, as the Senate said, were complete and untouchable; the affections of the people depend on the people. After Marshall finished, he moved, and the House passed, the resolutions written by Henry Lee, one of Washington's cavalry officers, which end: ". . . to the memory of the MAN, first in war, first in peace, and first in the hearts of his countrymen."

Notes

For a figure not thought of as literary, Washington left a mass of paper. We are between scholarly editions of it—the *Writings of George Washington,* edited by John C. Fitzpatrick (Washington, D.C.: 1931–39, 39 vols.), and the *Papers of George Washington,* edited by W. W. Abbot, Dorothy Twohig, *et al.* (Charlottesville, Virginia: 1983–   ). In the notes below, I have simply supplied dates and, when I am quoting letters, recipients. Much of his correspondence as Commander in Chief and President was drawn up with the help of aides, but the tone is consistent throughout, and, as Mrs. Liston noted, "he has always written better than the gentleman to whom the merit of his letters was ascribed."

John Marshall fought under Washington and was urged by him to get into politics. His biography, rigid with veneration, reads as if it were chiseled, rather than written. But he quotes from some papers—such as Washington's thoughts immediately before his first inauguration—which were subsequently lost.

As a baby, Washington Irving was carried by a Scottish maid into a shop after the president. "Please, your honor, here's a bairn was named after you," she said, and the elder Washington touched his head. Irving's biography was written at the end of his life, in a heroic struggle against failing health, out of a sense of patriotic obligation. It is an easier read than Marshall's, though rambling.

Both works are afflicted by gigantism: Marshall begins with Columbus's discovery of America and doesn't get his hero born until the beginning of volume two. It is as if nothing less than everything would do for their subject. This is also a problem with the standard modern biography, Douglas Southall Freeman's *George Washington* (New York: 1948–57, the seventh and last volume by John A. Carroll and Mary W. Ashworth—DSF in the notes). There are other problems. Freeman consistently underestimates Washington's intellectual and political sophistication. He also has a weird aversion to quotation. James Thomas Flexner's *George Washington* (Boston: 1965–72—JTF in the notes) is shorter (four volumes) and more vivid. Flexner had been an art historian—excellent background for our most visual president.

Samuel Eliot Morison's 1932 essay, "The Young Man Washington," is still thought-provoking—wrong on some things (religion, Sally Fairfax), dead right on others (the importance of horsemanship). More recently, Garry Wills's *Cincinnatus: George Washington and the Enlightenment* (1984) is a subtle and eloquent analysis of the role of resignation in Washington's career, almost obscured in a blizzard of art criticism. Richard Norton Smith's *Patriarch* (1993) focuses on his presidency. Paul K. Longmore's *The Invention of George Washington* (1988), which takes him up to 1775, is the best modern study and an invaluable corrective to Freeman.

George Washington: A Collection, compiled and edited by William B. Allen (Indianapolis: 1988) is an excellent one-volume anthology of Washington's writing, and Saul K. Padover's *The Washington Papers* (New York: 1955) can still be found in secondhand shops.

Introduction

1. Helen A. Cooper, *John Trumbull: The Hand and Spirit of a Painter* (New Haven: Yale University Art Gallery, 1983), p. 3.

2. *Ibid.,* p. 120.

3. GW to Joseph Reed, July 4, 1780.

4. JTF, Vol. IV, p. 493.

5. John Marshall, *The Life of George Washington* (New York: Wm. H. Wise & Co., 1925), Vol. II, p. 1.

6. Mason Locke Weems, *A History of the Life and Death, Virtues and Exploits of General George Washington* (Cleveland: The World Publishing Company, 1965), pp. 9–10. This was not a scholarly/ironic edition, but the real thing, 164 years old, and still going strong.

7. GW to Sarah Cary Fairfax, May 16, 1798; Samuel Eliot Morison, *By Land and By Sea* (New York: Alfred A. Knopf, 1953), pp. 178, 180.

8. John Keane, *Tom Paine: A Political Life* (Boston: Little, Brown and Company, 1995), p. 430.

9. Michael Winerip, "In School," *The New York Times,* April 27, 1994.

10. Paul K. Longmore, *The Invention of George Washington* (Berkeley: University of California Press, 1989), p. 204.

War

1. JTF, Vol. II, p. 97.

2. John C. Dann, *The Revolution Remembered* (Chicago: University of Chicago Press, 1980), p. 50; Henry P. Johnston, *The Campaign of 1776 Around New York and Brooklyn* (New York: Da Capo Press, 1971), p. 52.

3. Joseph Plumb Martin, edited by George F. Scheer, *Private Yankee Doodle* (Boston: Little, Brown and Company, 1962), pp. 32–34.

4. JTF, Vol. II, p. 123; GW to The President of Congress, September 17, 1776; Ambrose Serle, *The American Journal of Ambrose Serle* (San Marino, California: Huntington Library, 1940), p. 104.

5. Longmore, p. 158.

6. *The Life and Selected Writings of Thomas Jefferson,* Adrienne Koch

and William Peden, ed. (New York: Random House, 1944), p. 43; Longmore, pp. 146, 162.

7. JTF, Vol. I, p. 343.

8. GW to John Augustine Washington, May 31, 1754; to Robert Dinwiddie, June 3, 1754; Longmore, p. 24.

9. *Ibid.,* p. 30.

10. Morison, p. 176.

11. JFT, Vol. I, p. 341.

12. GW to The President of Congress, September 24, 1776.

13. GW to the President of Congress, September 8, 1776.

14. GW to Lund Washington, September 30, 1776.

15. JTF, Vol. II, p. 129.

16. *Op. cit.,* pp. 158–159.

17. *Op. cit.,* p. 162.

18. Thomas Paine, *Collected Writings,* Eric Foner, ed. (New York: The Library of America, 1995), p. 94.

19. Dann, p. 146.

20. JTF, Vol. II, p. 177.

21. *Pennsylvania Magazine of History and Biography,* XX, p. 517.

22. C. C. Haven, *Thirty Days in New Jersey Ninety Years Ago* (Trenton, 1867), p. 38.

23. *Ibid.,* p. 52.

24. Dann, p. 47; DSF, Vol. IV, p. 352.

25. JTF, Vol. II, pp. 185–187.

26. *Ibid.,* p. 237; Jeremiah Greenman, *Diary of a Common Soldier in the American Revolution, 1775–1783,* Robert C. Bray and Paul E. Bushnell, eds. (De Kalb: Northern Illinois University Press, 1978), p. 123; Robert Leckie, *George Washington's War* (New York: HarperCollins, 1992), p. 483; JTF, Vol. II, pp. 305–306; Alexander Hamilton, *The Basic Ideas of Alexander Hamilton,* Richard B. Morris, ed. (New York: Pocket Books, 1956), p. 35.

27. GW to Brigadier General Thomas Nelson, August 20, 1778.

28. GW to the President of Congress, September 24, 1776.

29. Clare Brandt, *The Man in the Mirror: A Life of Benedict Arnold* (New York: Random House, 1994), pp. 133, 139.

30. GW to Richard Henry Lee, March 6, 1777.

31. JTF, Vol. II, pp. 200, 241; GW to Benjamin Harrison, December 18, 1778; GW, General Orders, April 6, 1780.
32. Hamilton, p. 41; GW to James McHenry, July 22, 1798; Brandt, p. 236.
33. JTF, Vol. II, p. 407.
34. GW, General Orders, January 30, 1781; Circular to the New England States, January 5, 1781.
35. *Ibid.*, JTF, Vol. II, p. 399.
36. JTF, Vol. II, p. 63.
37. Lewis Nicola to GW, May 22, 1782.
38. For Trumbull and Charles Edward Stuart, see Cooper, p. 26; for Gorham and Prince Henry of Prussia, see Forrest McDonald, *The American Presidency: An Intellectual History* (Lawrence: University Press of Kansas, 1994), p. 151; GW to Lewis Nicola, May 22, 1782.
39. JTF, Vol. II, pp. 503–504.
40. GW to John Bannister, April 21, 1778.
41. GW, Speech to the Officers of the Army, March 15, 1783; Marshall, Vol. IV, p. 91.
42. GW, Address to Congress on Resigning his Commission, December 23, 1783.

Constitution

1. Robert Hunter, Jr., Louis B. Wright, and Marion Trinling, eds., *Quebec to Carolina in 1785–1786* (San Marino, California: The Huntington Library, 1943), p. 196.
2. GW to Francis Hopkinson, May 16, 1785; *Men and Times of the Revolution; or, Memoirs of Elkanah Watson* (New York: Dana & Co., 1856), p. 244; JTF, Volume III, p. 52.
3. Hunter, p. 193; Watson, p. 246; DSF, Vol. VI, p. 15; JTF, Vol. III, p. 82.
4. Glenn A. Phelps, *George Washington and American Constitutionalism* (Lawrence: University Press of Kansas, 1993), p. 75.
5. GW to Lafayette, July 25, 1785.
6. GW to James Warren, October 7, 1785.

7. GW to Benjamin Harrison, March 4, 1783; Circular to the States, June 14, 1783.
8. Jefferson, p. 436.
9. GW to James Madison, November 5, 1786; to David Humphreys, December 26, 1786; to Henry Lee, October 31, 1786.
10. Madison's survey was reworked as numbers 18, 19, and 20 of *The Federalist,* from which these quotes are taken. *The Federalist Papers,* Clinton Rossiter, ed. (New York: New American Library, 1961), pp. 133, 135.
11. GW to Edmund Randolph, December 21, 1786; to James Madison, December 16, 1786; to Henry Knox, April 2, 1787.
12. GW to Henry Knox, February 3, 1787; to John Jay, March 10, 1787; JTF, Vol. III, p. 107.
13. GW to Edmund Randolph, March 28, 1787; JTF, Vol. III, p. 111.
14. GW to Arthur Lee, May 20, 1787.
15. JTF, Vol. III, p. 116.
16. James Madison, *Debates in the Federal Convention of 1787,* James McClellan and M. E. Bradford, eds. (Richmond, Virginia: James River Press, 1989), pp. 25–26.
17. Max Farrand, *The Records of the Federal Convention* (New Haven, Connecticut: Yale University Press, 1937), Appendix A, pp. 87–97.
18. Madison, p. 46.
19. Farrand, pp. 86–87.
20. Farrand, pp. 469–471; Madison, pp. 203–204.
21. GW to James Madison, March 31, 1787; Phelps, p. 98.
22. GW to James Madison, March 31, 1787; GW, Summary of Letters from Jay, Knox, and Madison; Madison, p. 35.
23. *Ibid.,* pp. 161–163, 232, 235.
24. *Ibid.,* p. 90.
25. *Ibid.,* pp. 424–427.
26. Farrand, pp. 396–397; GW to Bushrod Washington, November 10, 1787; to David Stuart, November 30, 1787; Jefferson, p. 61.
27. Madison, p. 121.
28. *Ibid.,* pp. 616–617.
29. *Ibid.,* pp. 617–620.

30. *The Federalist Papers,* p. 513.
31. GW to Alexander Hamilton, August 28, 1788; to Thomas Johnson, April 20, 1788.
32. Farrand, p. 294.
33. *Ibid.,* p. 302.
34. DSF, Vol. VI, p. 140.
35. GW to Alexander Hamilton, October 3, 1788; GW to Henry Knox, April, 1798; to Alexander Hamilton, August 28, 1788.
36. GW to Alexander Hamilton, August 28 and October 3, 1788.
37. Madison, pp. 190, 228; GW to Lafayette, June 19, 1788.
38. JTF, Vol. III, p. 173.
39. *Ibid.,* pp. 177–178.

President

1. JTF, Vol. III, pp. 181, 188; GW, First Inaugural, April 30, 1789.
2. McDonald, p. 213.
3. Susan Gray Detweiler, *George Washington's Chinaware* (New York: Harry N. Abrams, Inc., 1982), pp. 108–112; JTF, Vol. III, pp. 195, 209.
4. GW to David Stuart, June 15, 1790; Jefferson, p. 130; JTF, Vol. III, p. 195.
5. *Ibid.,* pp. 216–217.
6. GW to Gouverneur Morris, Jan. 28, 1792; Richard Norton Smith, *Patriarch* (Boston: Houghton Mifflin, 1993), pp. 131–132; Page Smith, *John Adams* (Garden City: Doubleday and Co., 1962), p. 1084.
7. Richard Norton Smith, pp. 274, 97.
8. Marshall Smelser, "The Federalist Period as an Age of Passion," *American Quarterly,* X (Winter 1958), pp. 391–419.
9. JTF, Vol. III, p. 253; GW to Lafayette, June 10, 1792.
10. GW to Thomas Jefferson, August 23, 1792; Thomas Jefferson, *Papers* (Princeton, New Jersey: Princeton University Press, 1990), Vol. XXIV, p. 358.
11. Stanley Elkins and Eric McKitrick, *The Age of Federalism* (New York: Oxford University Press, 1993), pp. 290–292.

12. JTF, Vol. III, pp. 378–379.

13. Elkins and McKitrick, p. 468.

14. Thomas P. Slaughter, *The Whiskey Rebellion* (New York: Oxford University Press, 1986), p. 187; Elkins and McKitrick, p. 475.

15. *Ibid.,* pp. 478–481.

16. *Ibid.,* pp. 475–476.

17. JTF, Vol. IV, p. 174.

18. Slaughter, p. 215; JTF, Vol. IV, p. 185.

19. Slaughter, p. 191.

20. GW, Proclamation, September 25, 1794; to Charles Mynn Thruston, August 10, 1794.

21. GW, Message to Congress, November 19, 1794.

22. Elkins and McKitrick, p. 356; William Cobbett, *Peter Porcupine in America,* David A. Wilson, ed. (Ithaca, New York: Cornell University Press, 1994), pp. 198, 211.

23. Jefferson, p. 126.

24. Cobbett, p. 104.

25. Elkins and McKitrick, p. 125.

26. GW to Henry Laurens, November 17, 1778; Simon Schama, *Citizens* (New York: Alfred A. Knopf, 1989), p. 28.

27. GW to Alexander Hamilton, July 29, 1795.

28. *Ibid.*

29. Elkins and McKitrick, p. 425.

30. Farrand, p. 95.

31. GW to Edmund Randolph, July 29, 1795; to Alexander Hamilton, July 29, 1795.

32. Madison, p. 565.

33. GW, Message to the House, March 30, 1796.

34. Elkins and McKitrick, p. 448.

35. *Ibid.,* p. 517.

36. JTF, Vol. IV, pp. 296, 303; GW, Farewell Address, September 19, 1796.

37. Marshall, Vol. V, pp. 399–400.

38. Benjamin West to Rufus King, May 3, 1797 (this letter was pointed out to me by William Allen); Robert E. Spiller, *et al., A*

Literary History of the United States (New York: Macmillan, 1963), p. 200.

39. GW to Hames McHenry, September 14, 1798; to Patrick Henry, January 15, 1799; to John Adams, Feb. 1, 1799; to James McHenry, November 17, 1799.

Nature

1. JTF, Vol. I, pp. 191–192, or DSF, Vol. III, p. 6.
2. JTF, Vol. IV, p. 353.
3. JTF, Vol. II, pp. 40, 306.
4. JTF, Vol. III, p. 378; Longmore, p. 182; Richard Norton Smith, p. 47.
5. JTF, Vol. II, p. 13.
6. JTF, Vol. I, p. 317; Garry Wills, *Cincinnatus: George Washington and the Enlightenment* (Garden City, New York: Doubleday, 1984), xxii; Richard Norton Smith, p. 6.
7. JTF, Vol. III, p. 229.
8. Jefferson, p. 174; George W. P. Custis, Esq., "Washington A Sportsman," *American Turf Register and Sporting Magazine,* September 1829, pp. 7–8; GW, Diary for 1769.
9. See Jefferson's last letter, June 24, 1826 (Jefferson, p. 729).
10. JTF, Vol. I, p. 145; Vol. IV, p. 416.
11. Henry David Thoreau, *Walden* (New York: Harper & Row, 1958), p. 17; George Orwell, *The Collected Essays* (New York: Harcourt Brace Jovanovich, 1968), Vol. 3, p. 71.
12. Longmore, p. 182.
13. On Lee and Arnold, see John C. Fitzpatrick, *George Washington Himself* (Indianapolis: The Bobbs Merrill Company, 1933), p. 124; GW to Francis Hopkinson, February 5, 1789; JTF, Vol. III, p. 200.
14. JTF, Vol. IV, pp. 149, 46.
15. Richard Norton Smith, p. 305.
16. *Ibid.,* p. 4; TJF, Vol. I, pp. 100–101.
17. Hamilton, pp. 374–375.

18. JTF, Vol. IV, p. 67.
19. Elkins and McKitrick, p. 431; Jefferson, p. 174.
20. JTF, Vol. III, p. 217.
21. Richard Norton Smith, p. 263.

Morals

1. Benjamin Franklin, *The Autobiography and Other Writings* (New York: Bantam, 1982), p. 81; Elkins and McKitrick, p. 50.
2. *The Federalist Papers,* p. 71; Farrand, p. 85.
3. Sir Roger L'Estrange, Knt., *Seneca's Morals; by way of abstract* (London: Sherwood, Neely and Jones, 1818), pp. 61, 259, 269; William Fairfax to GW, September 5, 1754.
4. Doctor Johnson, *Prose and Poetry* (Cambridge: Harvard University Press, 1967), p. 878.
5. Joseph Addison, "Cato," in Ricardo Quintana, ed., *Eighteenth Century Plays* (New York: Random House, 1952), pp. 12, 20–21, 11.
6. L'Estrange, p. 90.
7. Addison, pp. 39–40, 46.
8. GW, to Thomas Jefferson, August 1, 1786.
9. Elkins and McKitrick, p. 517.
10. For a discussion of the origins of the rules, see Charles Moore, ed., *George Washington's Rules of Civility and Decent Behavior* (Boston: Houghton Mifflin, 1926).
11. GW to Earl of Loudon, January 1757.
12. Edmund Burke, *Reflections on the Revolution in France* (New York: Holt, Rinehart and Winston, 1959), p. 91.
13. Weems, pp. 352–353.
14. See McDonald, pp. 217–218.
15. GW to Martha Washington, June 18, 1775.
16. GW to Lund Washington, September 30, 1776.
17. GW to Henry Knox, March 8, 1787; to James Madison, May 20, 1792.
18. GW to Theodorick Bland, April 4, 1783; to Thomas Jefferson,

July 6, 1796; to James Madison, November 5, 1786; Message to Congress, November 19, 1794.

19. GW to Lafayette, May 28, 1788. For Barlow, see Henry Adams, *The United States in 1800* (Ithaca, New York: Cornell University Press, 1955, pp. 73–75.

20. Walt Whitman, *Leaves of Grass* (New York: New American Library, 1980), p. 245.

Ideas

1. GW to David Humphreys, July 25, 1785; Jefferson, p. 174; Longmore, p. 213.

2. Hamilton, p. 394.

3. GW to Thomas Jefferson, March 15, 1795.

4. GW to George Mason, April 5, 1769.

5. GW to Bryan Fairfax, August 24, 1774.

6. Jefferson, p. 719; Morris, p. 9.

7. See the Notes to the first edition of Morison's "The Young Man Washington" (Cambridge, 1932), p. 40.

8. Morison (Cambridge), p. 37; Longmore, p. 217.

9. GW, General Orders, July 4, 1775; to the Hebrew Congregations of the City of Savannah, Georgia (undated); Talk to the Cherokee Nation, August 29, 1796; Richard Norton Smith, p. 106.

10. GW to Robert Jackson, August 2, 1755.

11. GW to John Augustine Washington, July 4, 1778; General Orders, October 20, 1781; to Edmund Randolph, August 26, 1792; to Brigadier General Thomas Nelson, August 20, 1778.

12. GW to the Hebrew Congregation in Newport, August 7, 1790.

13. GW to Lafayette, July 5, 1785.

14. Morison, p. 168.

15. See the first chapter of Dorothy Lipson, *Freemasonry in Federalist Connecticut, 1789–1835* (Princeton, New Jersey: Princeton University Press, 1977).

16. Lipson, pp. 316–317.

17. Paul Leicester Ford, *Washington and the Theater* (New York: Benjamin Bloom, 1967), p. 41.
18. *Ibid.*, pp. 17, 26, 29, 49–50.
19. *Ibid.*, pp. 27–28, 36.
20. GW to Lafayette, April 5, 1783; General Orders, April 18, 1783.
21. Longmore, pp. 154–156.
22. GW to Jonathan Trumbull, March 3, 1797.

Fathers

1. Longmore, p. 204.
2. L'Estrange, p. 5.
3. GW to Benjamin Harrison, March 21, 1781; Richard Norton Smith, p. 4.
4. GW to Charles Thomson, January 22, 1784.
5. GW to the Rev. Jonathan Boucher, May 20, 1768; to John Parke Custis, February 28, 1781; Richard Norton Smith, p. 25.
6. Jefferson, p. 414; JTF, Vol. II, p. 218.
7. GW to Lieutenant Colonel Tench Tilghman, April, 24, 1783; Circular to the States, June 14, 1783.
8. See Morison (Cambridge), p. 36. The sermon was delivered by the Reverend Benjamin Stevens of Kittery, Maine (then Massachusetts). Stevens quoted Gilbert West's translation of the *Menexenus* (247b), attributed to Plato.

Patriarchs and Masters

1. Paine, pp. 206–207.
2. The modern view of the impact of Henry St. John, Viscount Bolingbroke, and the rest of the "country party" on the American Revolution was pioneered by Bernard Bailyn in 1965. Now it has become a commonplace. The "country party" were the opponents of the "court party" of Robert Walpole. They were divided into a libertarian wing, whose leading spokesmen

were John Trenchard and Thomas Gordon, authors of the *Cato* letters, and a Tory wing, whose chief publicist was Bolingbroke. In my view, the importance of Bolingbroke has been oversold. Perhaps because of my experience as a political journalist, he strikes me as an especially obvious fraud. He didn't strike his contemporaries that way, but we are not obliged to be deceived. Ideas that are insincerely held can be influential, but their influence will be less deep than those who bandy them about imagine. Bolingbroke's (mistaken) description of checks and balances in the English constitution found its way into Montesquieu, and hence back to America, but probably the main transatlantic legacy of the country party, left and right, was the paranoid style in American politics.

A better way to get a feel for the psychology of the Tory wing of the country party is by reading William Thackeray's *Henry Esmond* and *The Virginians.*

3. For Bolingbroke and his life, see Isaac Kramnick, *Bolingbroke and His Circle* (Cambridge, Massachusetts: Harvard University Press, 1968). "Caleb D'Anvers" [Henry St. John, Viscount Bolingbroke], *The Craftsman* (London: R. Francklin, 1731), Vol. VI. pp. 251–252; Vol. V, p. 156.

4. *The Works of the Late Right Honorable Henry St. John, Lord Viscount Bolingbroke* (London: 1777), Vol. III, pp. 82–83.

5. Longmore, p. 186.

6. *The Works,* pp. 76–77.

7. Sir Robert Filmer, ed. Johann P. Sommerville, *Patriarcha and Other Writings* (Cambridge, England: Cambridge University Press, 1991), pp. 5, viii.

8. *Ibid.,* p. 7.

9. *Ibid.,* pp. 16, 11, 4.

10. For Filmer's Virginian connections, see Peter Laslett, "Sir Robert Filmer, The Man and The Whig Myth," *William and Mary Quarterly,* Vol. V, 1948. For Byrd, see Longmore, p. 4.

11. Dumas Malone, *Jefferson the Virginian* (Boston: Little, Brown and Company, 1948), p. 255.

12. Laslett, p. 522; Jonathan Boucher, *A View of the Causes and Consequences of the American Revolution in Thirteen Discourses* (New York: Atheneum House, 1967), pp. 523–525.

13. Samuel Johnson, Political Writings (New Haven, Connecticut: Yale University Press, 1971), p. 454; Cobbett, p. 108.

14. GW to George William Fairfax, June 10, 1774; to Bryan Fairfax, July 20, 1774; to Bryan Fairfax, August 24, 1774; to Joseph Reed, December 15, 1775; Martin, p. 241.

15. Hamilton, p. 344; GW to Henry Laurens, March 20, 1779.

16. GW to Robert Morris, April 12, 1786.

17. GW to Lafayette, May 10, 1786.

18. JTF, Vol. IV, pp. 432–434.

19. *Ibid.,* p. 441; TJF, Vol. III, p. 24.

20. GW to Alexander Spotswood, November 23, 1794.

21. GW to Arthur Young, December 12, 1793; to Tobias Lear, May 6, 1794.

22. Madison, pp. 477–479, 392.

23. The man who did the rummaging was the sprightly defender of slavery, George Fitzhugh. See C. Vann Woodward, "George Fitzhugh, *Sui Generis,*" introduction to George Fitzhugh, *Cannibals All! or, Slaves Without Masters* (Cambridge: Harvard University Press, 1960).

Father of His Country

1. GW to Lafayette, June 19, 1788.

2. "The Spirit Ariel" in Rainier Marie Rilke, *Selected Poems,* J. B. Leishman, trans. (London: The Hogarth Press, 1945), p. 57.

3. GW, Circular to the States, June 14, 1783.

4. Henry Adams, *The Education of Henry Adams* (Boston: Houghton Mifflin Company, 1961), pp. 47–48; Jefferson, p. 174.

5. Longmore, p. 204.

Death

1. GW to Jonathan Trumbull, August 30, 1799.
2. Saul K. Padover, *The Washington Papers* (New York: Harper & Brothers, 1955), p. 1.
3. JTF, Vol. IV, pp. 457, 459; Richard Norton Smith, p. 354.
4. Marshall, Vol. V, pp. 368, 364.

Index